Walks in
Perthshire

Clan Walk Guides

Walks in Perthshire

Mary Welsh

**Maps and Illustrations by
Christine Isherwood**

First Published by Westmorland Gazette 1992

New Revised Edition Published by Clan Books 2000

ISBN 1 873597 09 6
Text © Mary Welsh 2000
Maps and Illustrations © Christine Isherwood 2000

Clan Book Sales Ltd
Clandon House
The Cross, Doune
Perthshire
FK16 6BE

Printed by
Cordfall Ltd, Glasgow

Publishers' Note

The second edition of this popular book contains a number of enjoyable new walks and other routes have been pleasingly extended as more paths have been opened up. The location map has been redrawn to the boundaries of the original county of Perthshire, instead of the arbitrary and probably short-lived borders arising from a series of local government revisions over the past twenty or thirty years. Returning the county to its original shape should please the majority of local inhabitants (and the Post Office), who consider that the towns and villages from Dunblane through to Tyndrum still belong to Perthshire. In this book we have used the old boundaries and this has enabled us to include walks based on places such as Callander, Doune and Lochearnhead.

The book has been thoroughly updated and the routes re-walked. If in spite of this, readers find anything incorrect or misleading in the text we shall be glad to be informed for future reference. However, it must be stated that the book sets out to be an entertaining and helpful guide, and neither the author nor the publishers can be held responsible for any loss or injury that might be considered to result from its use.

Finally, we would set down our delight to have Mary Welsh's eleven Scottish Walks titles under our own imprint and published in Scotland (Perthshire, to be sure!) and also to have in this edition the indispensable enhancement of maps and illustrations by her talented friend and collaborator, Christine Isherwood.

County of Perthshire

Contents

The Crags and Bracklinn Falls, Callander

Park in the riverside car park on the south side of Callander's Main Street, grid ref. 626079.

Callander The small Scots town was laid out in the 18th century and lies at the junction of the rivers Teith and Leny. The town will be familiar to those visitors who once viewed the television series Dr Finlay's Casebook in which it was given the name of Tannochbrae. Two of the several scenic walks from Callander are to Callander Crags and to the Bracklinn Falls; these have been combined in this walk.

Bracklin Falls, Callander

1. From the car park, return to the street. Turn left and, remaining on the same side of the road, walk on in the direction of The Trossachs and Crianlarich. Ignore the cycleway going off left, and here cross the road to go down a turning by the Tulipan Lodge Hotel. Follow a signpost, sometimes obscured by foliage in the summer, directing you left for 'The Crags and Wood Walks'.

2. Immediately beyond a Forestry Commission (FC) sign, turn left for the Crags walking the newly-constructed footpath which starts uphill at a steady gradient. This level-surfaced and well drained track could easily be mistaken for a forestry vehicle road, if it were a metre or so wider. It replaces the eroded old route of ascent marked on all the maps as hugging the course of an old wall. Soon the new walkway merges into the traditional path and the views start to open out, with, to the west and north, Ben Ledi close and majestic.

Then through widening gaps in the trees you have fine southern views over Callander and towards the upper Forth Valley and the Campsie Fells.

3. Then the path continues with all the characteristics of a mountain ridge-walk, entailing minor scrambles up and down rocky steps. The high point is marked by a substantial cairn erected in 1897 to mark Queen Victoria's Diamond Jubilee. The panoramic view fills in all the gaps from the earlier glimpses; Loch Venachar and the Trossachs to the west, Stuc a' Chroin and Ben Vorlich to the north. To the east, on a clear day, there is a fine prospect over Stirling with, spread out in a line, the castle, Wallace Monument and the little hill of Dumyat.

4. Continue along the ridge, which descends gradually at first and then more steeply. Finally, the path drops through dense woodland to a single-track road. Walk left for half a mile until just before you reach a gate across it.

5. Turn right down a forestry track to cross the Keltie Water by a simple bridge. Beneath it the burn starts to tumble through a series of pools and rocky cauldrons before disappearing into closely planted trees. From the bridge, look upstream to see the folds and ridges of the upper glen, culminating in Beinn Each on the skyline. Go on to climb the slope and, when the track makes a hairpin bend to the left, leave it and go ahead along a level grassy track.

6. Just before you cross a stone bridge, a gap in the trees on the right gives you a glimpse of the ridge you have recently walked, with Ben Ledi beyond. Carry on to a gate into farmland.

7. Beyond, continue to a tubular steel gate, with a corrugated-roofed steading over to the left. Here the track ends. Go through the steel gate and turn sharp right down a faint path which keeps close to a broken-down wall augmented by a modern sheep-wire fence. At the bottom, when you reach

Meadow Cranesbill

the trees, negotiate two fences and a burn to the right, to find an iron gate into woodland.

8. Pass through and down a few paces to join a path coming up from the left. Follow this to the right, where you will have an occasional glimpse of the Keltie Water far down the steep slope on your left. As you go you will hear the constant roar of the Bracklinn Falls crashing down the hollowed-out rocks long before you arrive at the fine vantage point, with the falls both above and below you. Even during a dry summer, this is an impressive sight; after a long, wet spell it is utterly awe-inspiring.

9. Cross the modern footbridge (stronger and safer than the rickety wooden structure which Sir Walter Scott is reputed to have ridden across to win a bet) then climb steps to a gain a level path. This takes you along an open stretch and then through woodland to the road, walked earlier but higher up on the route.

10. Go on (left), ignoring a turning to a reservoir, and then turn right into the woods at a FC sign. Fork left off the main forestry track with its vehicle access barrier. When the way divides, take the straight-ahead route through the woodland.

11. Climb steps to cross a footbridge, descending by more steps on the other side and go on. Ignore the track on the right. This is signed by a red-striped marker post and denotes the start of 400 steps to the top of the Crags. The woodland way descends steadily until you arrive at the point where you started to climb at the outset of the walk. Retrace your outward route to return to the car park.

Practicals

Type of walk: Good paths take you through woodland and on to the Crags above Callander, from where you can enjoy stunning views. The way then descends steadily and then on through more woodland to see the spectacular Bracklinn Falls—don't look down into the narrow chasm if you have vertigo!

Distance: 6 ½ miles
Time: 3 ½–4 hours
Maps: OS Landranger 57, OS Explorer 11

Doune Castle, the Ponds and Commonty Walk

To reach the castle car park, grid ref. 728012, enter the approach road from the direction of the town centre, rather than from the Dunblane road, because of the acute angle of turn. Go on past the church on the left, fork right after a narrow downward slope and then on along a road signposted to the castle. A visit to this fine castle is well worth while.

Doune and its Castle. Doune is one of Scotland's earliest burghs, with a charter granted by King James 1611. Its medieval castle is one of the best preserved in Scotland, which is not only steeped in history but has been much favoured by film-makers because of its well preserved walls and battlements, and its commanding site on a rocky outcrop above two rivers.

Doune Castle

Salmon spend their adult life in the sea. Then, at maturity they return to the quiet inland streams where they were spawned. To reach them they battle against rushing torrents to leap headlong up swift waterfalls or fish-ladders provided to help them scale impeding weirs. In the clear well-oxygenated water and gravelly beds of the streams the females lay their eggs and the males fertilise them, and soon afterwards the adults die. The eggs, sometimes 10,000 alone from one female, thrive in shallow fast-running water. In about two months or more the young burst forth from the eggs. They carry a huge yolk-sac, which nourishes them in the early weeks. Some months later they venture forth as free-swimming fry, and in about a year they set off downstream. After several years at sea they return, often to the same river where they hatched, probably drawn by memory of the smell.

Walk 2

The Castle Walk

1. Leave the castle and go down the cobbled approach road for a few steps. Swing left across the well tended grass to pick up a narrow path. This descends steeply to the left of a wall and then a fence to reach the banks of the River Teith by a kissing gate.

2. Do not go through the gate, but turn left along a narrow but well used path which undulates along the high bank of the fast-flowing Teith. Pass a fine deep pool, which briefly halts the speeding surface waters and in which local anglers still occasionally lure wild salmon.

3. On reaching an open area of more level ground continue close to the river. At this point, especially if you are an early morning visitor, you may hear the lions roaring for their breakfast in the woods of the Blair Drummond Safari Park.

4. At the confluence of the River Ardach with the Teith, go round and back along the bank of the tributary river. Follow the track past the castle on its rocky pedestal up to your left, and return to your car.

The Ponds and Commonty (Common land) Walk

Park in the car park on the north side of Doune, grid ref. 726018. To reach this leave the A820, on its north side, with the parish church on your right. Follow the signposted 'Nature Trail' to go over the bridge and turn left for 'Doune Ponds,' which takes you to the parking area.

1. Pick up a leaflet from a dispenser by the kissing gate. Beyond, go straight ahead, ignoring tracks to either side until you see the central pond ahead of you at a picnic area with a wooden platform by the pond. Here various species of duck, coot, moorhen and, occasionally swans, congregate, hoping to be fed.

2. With your back to the pond follow the track right which takes you round beside the pond. Pass a birdwatchers' hide and, bearing right past marker post 2, take the sometimes muddy pond-side track. A second hide is seen by the waymark post 3. The path now winds up into a conifer plantation. Ignore steps going down to the left and walk through trees to cross a wooden platform at marker post 4.

Coot and Waterlilies

13

Keep to the lower level route, which passes marker post 5 and descends into a grove of downy birch, where wild orchids may be found among the buttercups and wild strawberries. In the later months this is also a good spot for finding various fungi. Pass waymark 6, and when the path rises to a junction at marker 7, go ahead along a gravelled section until reaching open ground.

3. Here marker 8 directs you to the left through silver birch. Take the steps up the steep brae. At the top, press on ahead to join a rutted estate road going downhill for about 100m, then follow the signpost for the Commonty Walk uphill to the left. This soon becomes a terrace walk along a tree-lined track. To the right, fine views open up across Doune to the Carse of Stirling and the Campsie Fells, with Ben Lomond to the far right. Looking at this peaceful prospect, it is hard to believe that the vast Glasgow and Clydebank conurbation lies less than ten miles beyond the skyline.

4. On reaching a road, turn right and then follow the signposted 'Doune Trail' left along a track between conifer plantations. Before the track enters a field there are steps on the right taking you down a wide, level grassy track. Turn right again, and stride back towards Doune. This path takes you along the bed of the one time Callander and Oban railway. After emerging from a cutting, look for a gap in the low trees and bushes on your right for a glimpse of Ben Ledi, Callander's presiding mountain.

5. When you see the way fenced off ahead of you under an over-bridge, turn left past tennis courts, go through a metal gate onto the road, turn right and cross the bridge. You are now on the road you drove down earlier, and by turning left at the Doune Ponds signpost and walking a short distance you arrive at the car park.

Practicals

Type of walk: Two delightful walks close to the charming town of Doune.

Distance: Castle walk ¾ miles.
Time: ½ hour

Distance: Ponds and Commonty Walk: 3 ½ miles
Time : 1 ½ hours
Maps: OS Landranger 57, OS Pathfinder 370

14

Glen Ogle Trail

Park in the Lochearnhead public car park, grid ref. 593238. This lies opposite the Water Sports Centre and about a quarter of a mile along the A85 towards Comrie from the junction with the A84 coming up from Callander.

Callander and Oban Railway. The railway through Glen Ogle originally ran from Callander to Oban. Alas in 1965, the section from Callander to Crianlarich was closed after great boulders, torn by frost and heavy rain from the crags above Lochearnhead, created a massive landslide, blocking and damaging the track. The line was due to be axed by Dr Beeching and British Railways used this opportunity to bring forward the closure. At the time of this book going to press, the whole of the outward section of this walk, which uses the track-bed, is subject to 'upgrading' to form an essential part of National Cycle Route 7. Access may be restricted while this work is in progress until late summer 2000.

Viaduct, Glen Ogle

1. Walk the roadside footpath up to the above junction and turn right in the direction for Crianlarich. Where the footpath ends, just beyond the stub of a partly dismantled viaduct, cross the road with care and go up the old station approach road now signposted Lochearnhead Scout Station. This is the former Lochearnhead station which has been restored and converted for scouts. After a few steps, follow a cast iron metal signpost for the Glen Ogle Trail, which directs you steeply up through the trees to a gate through a high fence. This gives you access to the former railway track-bed perched on the hillside 91m/100yds up. (As you climb look back

16

for a good view over the village to Loch Earn and the hills beyond.) From this point and throughout, the Glen Ogle Trail is clearly waymarked by yellow arrows on short stakes.

2. Turn right along the track, now used as a cycle track as well as a walkers' route, and stride out along the steadily-rising evenly graded terrace through the trees that now surround it. Overhead you might spot a pair of buzzards circling on the thermals. The track continues to climb, coming to a section where the ravages of past severe winters are awesomely visible—a landslide in 1965 brought about the closure of the line.

3. Two miles on, the way crosses a fine curving stone viaduct across a deep corrie, then carves its way through the steep hillside with the glen narrowing towards its head and the main road drawing closer. At this point, just after crossing a concrete bridge over a burn, look out for a waymark up the bank to the right, directing the walker to a ladder-stile over the wire fence, the high point of the walk and the start of the path down.

4. This will be the turning point for some walkers. Others may wish to continue up the rail/cycle way, which passes under a stone arched bridge and goes straight on to reach a point where the road converges at an open area, used by vehicles as a layby. Here, down to the left, is the attractive Lochan Lairig Cheile, filling the watershed between Glen Ogle and Glen Dochart with its natural tree lined beauty. Carry on along the track and, immediately after passing the Glenogle Cottages, take a narrow path through the hedge on the right which leads up to a road.

Buzzard

5. Here you get a preview of the Ben Lawers skyline as you emerge, but for the best viewpoint, cross the road carefully and make for the parking and picnic area opposite, entered a few metres along to the right. Walk through the car park, where there is usually a mobile snack bar, and soon a glorious view of the whole of the Ben Lawers range spreads before you beyond Killin and the Tay valley. This is a rewarding place for your picnic.

6. To return, retrace your steps down the old railway and look out for the ladder-stile, now on your left, soon after passing under the arched over-bridge. The grassy and occasionally boggy track down the glen is generously waymarked with yellow arrows. The waters which combine to form the Ogle Burn are crossed by stepping stones and the way remains on the left bank. After prolonged rainfall, the waterfalls on the upper burn, which you pass, can be very impressive.

7. The track winds through trees and reaches a stile onto the A85. Go straight across to follow a narrow path which keeps well above the road and farm buildings. Two stiles and a tributary burn are crossed in quick succession and the track then continues, clearly waymarked, until a footbridge across the Ogle Burn leads back up to the road by the old railway viaduct. Retrace the roadside footpath route to the car.

Practicals

Type of walk: The trail includes a spectacular section of a dismantled railway line. Now the track-bed is an enjoyable walk for all the family with the return journey by way of a good path that winds its way down the glen.

Distance:	8 miles. With an extension to the Ben Lawers viewpoint 10 miles.
Time:	3 hours and 4 hours
Maps:	OS Landranger 51, Pathfinder 347

Linear walk from Edinample by Loch Earn via Stuc a' Chroin and Beinn Each to Ardchullarie More on Loch Lubnaig

This is a full-day linear walk, best attempted on a reliably clear day by a party of walkers with two cars. Park one car in the big layby found on the east side (right going north) of the A84, four miles south of Strathyre, grid ref. 585138, close to the farmhouse, Ardchullaric More.

Park the second car at Edinample, grid ref. 601226. This is reached by driving 8 miles north towards Lochearnhead, and then as you descend towards the loch and the village, look for the single track road, off right, signposted South Loch Earn Road. Follow this road to the hamlet of Edinample to park on the verge, on the right, before the bridge, ensuring that you do not obstruct the access to the track up the glen.

Stuc a' Chroin & Beinn Each from Glen Ogle

Edinample Falls. The Burn of Ample descends steeply, in three cascades, 20m/60ft in total, in the direction of Loch Earn. The cascades are a fine sight at any time, but are really dramatic after a prolonged wet spell.

Stuc a' Chroin the peak of harm or danger (not really if you take care). On a clear day the view from this Munro (see walk 40) is stunning. Stirling and the Forth estuary lie far away to the south-east, with the rounded Ochils above. The prospect eastwards is dramatically interrupted by the rocky top of Ben Vorlich close by. Then the eye can sweep around in an unbroken arc from Ben Lawers in the north, by Ben More and the high tops surrounding Crianlarich to Ben Lomond, behind and just to the right of Ben Ledi.

Corbetts. Between the two world wars, John Rooke Corbett was a keen member of the Scottish Mountaineering Club. He listed all those mountains that ranged in height between 762m and 915m (2500ft and 3000ft) and that had a drop of 153m/500ft around their summits. There are 221 mountains in his list including Beinn Each which is climbed on this walk.

1. Stride up the Glen Ample track, with the falls of Edinample on your left. Almost immediately the track divides and you take the left fork to continue steadily upward, close to the wooded banks of the Burn of Ample. Follow the track until it swings left over a bridge to the house of Glen Ample Here go on along the narrower path which continues on the left bank, with a deer fence on the right. Cross a burn by a wooden footbridge and take the red arrowed route up through the trees opposite. This gives access to the track coming out of the farm on the left, which you follow as it climbs through young but rapidly growing conifers.

2. Cross a stile and emerge from the trees on to the open hillside. From the continuing track there are fine and steadily expanding views of the high hills around, with the massive

bulk of Ben Vorlich ahead and above. Then the track suddenly peters out. Here continue ahead, following the main burn and then making for the lowest point of the skyline through the Coire Fuadarach and on to the saddle—Bealach an Dubh Choirein. Look and listen for red grouse as you go.

3. Join the climbers' track from the saddle, which steeply ascends to the base of the imposing rock face

Walk 4

of Stuc a' Chroin. The experienced scrambler may be tempted to seek a route directly up the crag, but the more cautious should turn right, on reaching the rocks, to take the steep but safe narrow path which starts upwards from about 50m/150ft to the north-west. This leads to the summit plateau of the great buttress. Follow the fence posts south to arrive at the summit cairn, 975m/3189ft.

4. Several ridges radiate from the summit plateau. It is important, especially if clouds come down unexpectedly, to ensure that you go on to leave the top, walking due west and with fence posts and an intermittent path marking the route along the winding ridge. This turns south and then west again, dropping to the Beallach Glas. Beyond this, the ridge establishes a southerly course as it rises to a knobbly but unnamed subsidiary summit.

5. Descend to the Beallach-nan-Cabar and then climb again to the summit of Beinn Each, 811m/2604ft, not a Munro but a Corbett.

6. From the summit take a faint path, descending the nose westwards, beside the line of fence posts. This turns down from the summit and leads to craggy outcrops. To avoid these bear left (south) down a steep slope to pick up the headwaters of the delightful Eas an Eoin, and follow this as it tumbles steeply down to the valley. Keep to the right (north) bank, where there are traces of a path.

7. On reaching the track, coming over the pass from Glen Ample, turn left and make for the plantation below. Beyond the forest fence the walkers' path down to Ardchullarie More diverges right from the forest track, keeping close to the burn on the right. Continue on to join the road. Turn right for a few steps to reach the layby.

Red grouse in heather

NB   The walk could be attempted by leaving a car at the Ardchullarie More layby, timing arrival there to enable you to take one of the occasional Stirling to Killin service buses, or a post bus which starts from Callander. Get off the bus at South Loch Earn Road junction and walk just less than a mile to the Glen Ample track. Check bus times at Rob Roy Tourist Centre, Callander (Tel. 01877 330342).

NB   For the two car walk, don't forget to take all your equipment and supplies for a long day for the whole party!

Practicals

Type of walk: A challenging, rewarding 10 mile walk. It starts with a pleasant riverside stroll up a wooded glen, it continues by ascending a wild corrie and culminates in a rocky scramble to the peak of a Munro. Then it goes on along a wide and winding ridge to the summit of a Corbett, followed by a steep descent to valley level. Do NOT attempt in the mist.

Distance: 10 miles
Time: 8 hours
Maps: Harveys Superwalker Ben Ledi (1-25,000),
OS Landrangers 51 and 57, OS Explorer 11,
OS Pathfinder 347

5

Goat's Path and Glentarken Wood, St Fillans

Park in a large layby at the east end of Loch Earn, west of St Fillans and beyond the Four Seasons Hotel, grid ref. 689246.

Neish Island. The island lies just off shore. This is a crannog or man-made island dating back to prehistoric lake-dwellers. In 1612 a particularly bloody massacre occurred when the island was occupied by the McNeishes. They allowed only their own boats on Loch Earn. Their traditional enemies were the McNabs from Killin. One night the McNeishes waylaid a McNab servant carrying provisions. A few days later the McNabs, under the cover of darkness, carried out a surprise attack on the island, and massacred all except one small boy. The severed head of the McNeish chieftain was carried back to Killin.

Viaduct,
Glentarken Path

Loch Earn. The lovely loch is surrounded by wooded hills and mountains. They rise steeply from the water's edge, with the high peaks of Ben Vorlich (1000m/3231ft) to the south and Ben More (1170m/3852ft) to the west. The loch is 10.5km/six and a half miles long and 88m/287ft deep though and its is said to be very much deeper in places. The bed of the loch drops almost vertically within a few feet of the shore.

Walk 5

1. Take the roadside path past the Four Seasons and go on to pass the Drummond Arms Hotel. As you go look for Neish Island, just off shore. Immediately beyond the hotel, turn left into Shoemaker's Lane and walk to the end. Go through the gateway and follow a narrow path bearing slightly right to pass through a small oak wood. Continue on the path through pasture to a gate. Turn left between the buttresses of the old railway embankment. Ignore the turning to the A-frame houses. Beyond, go left through a farm gate signposted Goat's Walk. The track ahead soon becomes a narrow path. Go off left through the bracken, with the path climbing gently, keeping parallel with the disused railway.

2. Beyond the next gate you now reach the Goat's Path; it is named after the wild goats that once grazed the pastures. Stroll the ascending path, enjoying the splendid views ahead of Loch Earn and its attendant mountains. From the fir plantation, to the right, come the quiet whisperings of goldcrests and coal tits. Go on along the path over the scree of Creag Mhor and on through, in mid

24

summer, heather, golden rod, harebells, bedstraw and foxgloves. Ahead the loch stretches away, breathtakingly lovely. Head into a plantation of firs and then, beyond, an open area with two seats well placed for enjoying the view. Continue through more firs to reach a track. Turn left and walk downhill. Cross the railway bridge and drop down to the track coming up from the lochside to the left. Bear right by a wooden garage and follow this track through deciduous woodland, with more views of Loch Earn. Cross a small burn and walk beside a two arched railway bridge. Walk on for 91m/100yds for access, on the right, to the old railway track. The wide stony way is shaded by young birch and you have delightful brief glimpses of the Loch.

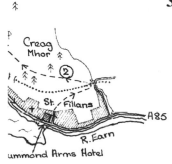

3. Cross a small viaduct, with a good view of a waterfall to your right and then a bridge with metal rails. Just beyond, on the right, take the narrow path that leads on, steadily upwards, through bracken and into Glentarken Wood. The way continues through alders and then deep into mixed woodland and comes to a burn. Cross by a stout wooden footbridge built by the Royal Engineer reservists in 1996.

4. Stride into oak woodland. This was once coppiced. Look for the many stems or stumps at the base of each tree. Head on along the path as it moves into firs before reaching a gate. Go ahead along a rather soft, muddy track where you will have to pick your own way. Emerge from the trees through a gateway, with the remains of a former iron kissing gate. All about lies the evidence of the deserted settlement of Easter Glentarken where twelve families lived before the Highland Clearances. Follow the indistinct track as it winds through bracken, Progress over another very wet path, helped on your way by grand views of Loch Earn.

5. Pass through a gate in the fence and cross a small burn. Beyond, drop down over the steepish slopes on the left. Very soon a narrow path becomes evident. Follow it downhill and, where it begins to swing left. Step over a stream, the same one crossed at the top of the slope. Climb the right hand fence onto the railway track and turn left to pass beneath a bridge. Beyond, a narrow path weaving through a jungle of nettles soon becomes a delightful track. To the left deciduous trees slope upwards and birch slope down towards the loch.

6. Cross the five-arched viaduct over the white topped waterfall and walk on, making a right turn to leave the track. Continue ahead to join the reinforced track that leads down the to the road (A85) by the loch. A few steps to the right takes you back to the parking layby.

Coal tit

Practicals

A pleasing generally easy walk with exciting views of a lovely loch and its surrounding hills and mountains.

Distance: 5 miles
Time: 3–4 hours
Maps: OS Landranger 51, Pathfinder 348

6

Glen Lednock, Comrie

Park in the Primary School car park at Comrie, grid ref. 773221

Comrie. Comrie is a Gaelic name, meaning 'confluence of streams'. The waters of Ruchill, the Earn and the Lednock come together at the village. The Romans occupied the area until the third century AD. Comrie suffered from the plague and from a small pox epidemic. Its people always considered itself a Highland village and in the past spoke Gaelic. They sympathised with the Jacobites but, unlike Crieff, the town was not burnt to the ground. It is famous as Britain's earthquake centre. It suffers mild earthquakes because it lies on the Highland Boundary Fault. Here two geological areas meet and even after many millions of years the two have not knitted together.

Shaky bridge
(now replaced)

Deil's Caldron means Devil's Kettle—an apt name for this hollow in the ravine where the Lednock has cut a narrow passage. Stones and sand carried by the burn swirl round and round, cutting a large kettle-shaped pothole. In time the river breaks through and plunges as a fall into another basin. Legend has it that it was the favourite haunt of a water elf who enticed victims down the huge pothole.

Melville Monument was built on the top of Dun More in 1811. It commemorates Lord Melville, Henry Dundas, who was chief minister in Scotland under William Pitt the younger. The obelisk is 22m/72ft high and, when it was struck by lightning in 1894, the steeplejack who repaired it, reported that from its summit he could see Castle Rock in Edinburgh.

Walk 6

1. From the car park go right along the main street until it turns sharply left. At this corner carry straight on up Monument Street which leads up Glen Lednock. In 183m/200yds turn right to follow a path that skirts a field. Soon the path curves round into the wooded glen. Continue on to take another path to the right. This is railed and leads down to a fenced viewing area above the Wee Caldron, a set of rapids, in a noisy hollow, which is shaded with oak, rowan and beech. Over the swirling water a tiny wren flits back and forth.

28

2. Return to the main way via a few steps and a narrow path and walk on. The path runs close to the road but does not join it. It continues past a hut to a railed wooden walkway and a series of wooden steps, which lead down to a platform over Deil's Caldron, the spectacular waterfall. Leave by another railed way which takes you up to the road. Turn right and after 50m take the signposted gated path on the left, where a narrow, partly-stepped way leads upwards through the conifers of Dun More. Towards the top, the path zig-zags through heather to the railed obelisk. The view is breathtaking. Look north to see Ben Chronzie. To its left stands the huge dam of Loch Lednock, specially reinforced to withstand earthquakes. Bright patches of blue to the west are the waters of Loch Earn.

3. On leaving the monument, go down beyond the first zig-zag in the trees to reach a point where an alternative track diverges from the ascent route. Continue on this, descending steadily through the forest in a northerly direction. Soon the track leaves the plantation by a gate, with a stile, and moves on to the open hillside. There is now a grand view across the Lednock valley and of the hills on either side. Follow the track until you can turn off to the right, descending fairly steeply, at first, to the road below.

4. A few steps along to the right will bring you to a waymark indicating a sharp turn back to the left for Laggan Wood, your return route to Comrie. This track leads downhill towards a footbridge known locally as 'Shaky Bridge', since the original structure was distinctly wobbly, being attached at the far end to the crook of a double-trunked sycamore. Unfortunately, this has now been replaced by a sturdy modern bridge: safer, but not so romantic.

Roe deer

5. Cross the bridge, turn right along the narrow path beside the alder-lined burn. Climb the stile and then the steps beyond that lead up a slope covered with bracken, Follow the waymarked wide grassy path. Look right to see Lord Melville's monument towering above the firs and birch that find a foothold on the almost sheer sides of the crag. A waymark directs you slightly left, away from the lovely river, then climbs steadily to a kissing gate into Laggan Wood. Go on through oak woodland to follow the path as it drops downhill with firs to the left and oak to the right. Look for the waymark where the firs crowd in on both sides. This directs you to a path on the right of the forest walk but still continuing ahead. Very soon you pass into more oak woodland, where you might see roe deer, and the path leads to a stepped and railed steep descent.

6. Before you descend, head on to a heather-clad clearing with a seat. From here you have a fine view over Comrie, and its white church with turreted steeple, built in 1804. Return and descend the steepish slope by the steps. Carry on along the path through mixed woodland. Where the path divides, take the one nearest to the river. Walk on with care to pass a weir and remain on the path nearest to the hurrying burn. Pass through a gap in a stone wall.

7. Cross a substantial wooden footbridge over the Lednock. Bear right to walk along the track bed of the old railway and follow the path until it meets a lane and the car park.

Practicals

This pleasing walk starts from an attractive village. It continues upstream of the a lovely river through a richly wooded gorge to two dramatic waterfalls. It visits a viewpoint with an enormous monument. Once the river is crossed the return along the glen, much of it wooded, is equally delightful.

Distance:	4 ½ miles/7.2km
Time:	3 hours
Maps:	OS Landranger 52, Pathfinder 348
Terrain:	Clear paths all the way but some can be steep and muddy.

7

Lady Mary's Walk and Laggan Hill, Crieff

Park in Taylor Park, grid ref. 858222. To reach this attractive grassy recreation area, drive north-west through the town centre following West High Street. At the junction, turn right, uphill, into Comrie Street. Take the first left into Milnab Street, which leads downhill to Taylor Park and ample parking spaces.

Crieff. In the 17th century Crieff was Perthshire's principal market town. Scotland's largest cattle sales were held here, the animals being driven from all over the Highlands. Many dealers came up from the south and the cattle were then herded on into England along drove roads that today are frequented by walkers. Then the south facing town became a fashionable Victorian health resort. Today it is the bustling 'capital' of Strathearn, the broad valley of the River Earn.

Lady Mary's Walk, Crieff

Lady Mary. She was Lady Mary Murray, the daughter of Sir Patrick Murray of Ochtertyre. The walk along the north bank of the River Earn, was created in 1815 by Sir Patrick and, because it was his daughter's favourite it was named after her. It also remains one of the favourite walks for the people of Crieff and its visitors.

Walk 7

1. Cross the bridge over the fast-flowing River Turret. Beyond, look left for the footpath sign for the walk. Stride along the tree-lined path, with the noisy burn to the left. To the right lie pastures. Pass between the pillars of an old bridge that once carried a railway line over the Turret to Loch Earn and beyond. Notice the embankment to the right where the line continued.

2. Follow the path, which in summer is lined with wood cranesbill, and the aromatic sweet cicely. Pass through a kissing gate and head along the glorious way. It then swings away from the Turret and comes beside the wide, stately River Earn, just west of the confluence. The path soon joins the wide way beneath a row of magnificent beech trees, with some lime, larch and scots pine. The wide, flat, easy-to-walk path continues for a mile, keeping close to the pleasing river, where dippers feed in the rapids and mallards dawdle in the shallows. Walk on where the track becomes a narrow path and follow it where it swings right away from the hurrying water to pass between two pillars of another defunct bridge.

3. At the T-junction of tracks, turn right for a few steps, and then go through a gate on the left to ascend a clear winding path which

keeps to the right-hand side of mixed woodland. Where it swings up to the right, follow it to a kissing gate and continue on the edge of woodland with a wire fence on the right. At the next gateway, bear right along a track coming in from the left. Soon the wooded top of Laggan Hill is reached, marked by a fine old wrought-iron seat, which was no doubt placed there when there was a wide panoramic view of Strathearn. Alas, the now mature conifers below have grown up to obscure the prospect, and walkers must hope for the day when some ruthless tree-felling will open it up again.

4. On the steady descent, there are very pleasant views over Crieff, with the Hydro complex high on the hill opposite, topped by the trees and the viewpoint of The Knock (see walk 8). The entrance to a disused quarry on the left is now so overgrown that you can easily pass it without realizing the extent of the former workings. The track makes it way down towards new houses on the outskirts of the town.

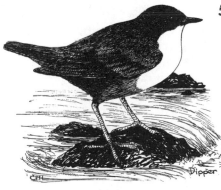

Dipper

5. On reaching a cross-road, with Turret Lodge on the left corner, and where the track ahead is signposted as another approach to Lady Mary's Walk, turn left along a narrow metalled road, keeping the row of tidy modern houses on your right. Go on to the end, then turn right downhill. Soon you pass the start of your walk, and cross the bridge over the Turret to regain the car park.

Practicals

A pleasing leisurely woodland walk beside the River Earn. Your return is over Laggan Hill.

Distance: 4 miles
Time: 2 hours
Maps: OS Landranger 52, Pathfinder 349
Terrain: Easy walking.

8

The Knock of Crieff

To reach the car park, grid ref. 864226, go up the narrow one-way Hill Street which has signposts for Crieff Hydro and Morrison's Academy. After widening for two-way traffic, the road becomes Ferntower Road. Drive to the top of this road, turn left and then immediately fork right, where there are signs for an intimidating range of Hydro destinations (suites, chalets, stables etc.) but no mention of the Knock. Press on and soon the lower of two car parks is reached.

The Knock is a large old red sandstone mound mainly covered in deciduous woodland. Its name 'Knock' comes from the Gaelic word for hill—'Cnoic'. It is 241m/793ft high.

Walk 8

Scots pine

1. Walk back a few metres, then go off left along a wide ride, with dense woodland on the left and fine views over Strathearn to the right. Keep along this route, ignoring tracks turning uphill. Soon you reach a new landmark, the Millennium Cairn erected for January 1, 2000. It is built in the beehive shape of a broch. The ruins of Ferntower, a house with an enviable viewpoint, lies to the right.

2. The ride begins to climb and curve left round the hill. After rounding the nose of the hill, follow the waymark to the right, directing you to a narrow track which detours to the right and gives access, over a wire fence, to an outstanding viewpoint. From a raised knoll next to the trunk of a dead conifer, you can look across the valley in which the delightfully named Shaggie Burn winds down between the picturesque hamlet of Monzie and Monzie Castle, and to see the bulk of the nearest Munro, Ben Chonzie, filling the middle distance. Over to the left, a fine panorama of the hills surrounding Strathearn open out, with Ben More seen in the background on a clear day.

3. Return to the path, go through the trees to the right, and join the main ride for a short distance until a fence and gateway are reached, as the track starts to descend. Here take a left turn along a rising footpath, forking to the right where it divides by another fence.

4. This pleasant, flower bedecked-path leads to the summit of the Knock and a substantial marble memorial plinth. The brass plate it supports identifies the main mountain tops you can see.

5. Leave by the track which continues ahead, westwards, and descends through mainly deciduous woodland to the car park.

View Indicator,
the Knock, Crieff

Practicals.

Type of walk: A short easy walk through woodland to a splendid viewpoint on the hill called the Knock, Crieff.

Distance: 2 ½ miles
Time: 1–1 ½ hours
Maps: OS Landranger 52, Pathfinder 349

9

The Oak Walk, Auchterarder

Park in the car park west of the Information Centre in the High Street of Auchterarder, grid ref. 946128.

Auchterarder (meaning high upland) nestles in farmland high above Strathearn and is famed for its lovely landscapes. It is a long linear town that lies against the Ochil Hills. Once it was the centre of the chain-mail industry in Scotland, providing armour for royal armies. In 1715 the Jacobite leader, the Earl of Mar, was forced to

The oak walk, Auchterarder

fall back on Perth. In his retreat he destroyed all food and shelter for the pursuing armies and Auchterarder was laid to waste. Below are some of the older spellings of the name of the town:

Eochteradeour, Uchterardour, Outread, Ochteraider

The oak tree has always been important in Great Britain. It touched man at every stage of life, from the cradle to coffin. It was used to provide charcoal for smelting ore. It was essential for building wooden warships particularly from the time of the Armada to Trafalgar. Its leaves and acorns are easily identified. In winter its many-scaled buds cluster at the tips of the twigs and when they open the twigs sprout in several directions, creating the crooked growth characteristic of the tree.

Walk 9

1. From the car park return to the High Street, cross and walk left until you reach Castleton Road. Turn right and walk on for half a mile, passing the Castleton village name-plate. Cross the road and take a farm track on the left, opposite a house named Park View. In the large fields on either side of the track grow barley and wheat. The track goes by Lower Borland Park, the site of a village that provided accommodation for soldiers disbanded at the end of the Seven Years War in 1763. From here look left to see the steep-sided round-topped Ochils and to the right, the hills and mountains beyond Crieff.

2. Where the track leads to a cottage, take the gate on the left. Beyond, a narrow grassy path leads to a small footbridge, which you cross. Walk onwards, keeping to the right of a fence, to a stile into the oak walk.

38

3. Turn left. Follow the narrow, easy-to walk path between the lovely oaks. Beech, ash, scots pine and sweet chestnut also flourish in this narrow strip of woodland. Beyond the trees stretch fields of cereals. Pass through a kissing gate to continue along the path, through pasture, where in August knapweed and scabious flower. Follow the way as it passes through more splendid oaks and comes to another kissing gate.

4. Beyond, turn left and walk along Tullibardine Road. Where it joins Orchil Road, look for the cairn, commemorating Queen Victoria's Diamond Jubilee. Continue along Orchil Road (east) to Townhead. Turn left along the High Street to return to your car.

Oak

Practicals

A short low-level walk through farmland and woodland.

Distance:	2 miles
Time:	1 hour
Maps:	OS Landranger 58, Pathfinder 360
Terrain:	Easy all the way.

10

A Walk in Abernethy Glen

Park in Abernethy's free 'Inn Close' car park, grid ref. 189164. This modest space has no signpost from the High Street, and to find it drive from the east side of the town, past the post office and inn. Turn sharp left up a narrow road, then left again into the parking area behind the building from which it takes its name.

Abernethy lies in a fold of the Ochils overlooking the fertile plains of the Earn and the Tay. It is a gracious old town with houses that front onto the street. It was once an important Pictish settlement and it has a well preserved round tower. This was believed to have been constructed in the 9th century. It was used for keeping watch against marauders, as a sanctuary in time of trouble and a place to store valuables and records. A spiral staircase was put in at a later date and a clock added. Look for the metal collar

Round Tower, Abernethy

C. M. Isherwood

(jougs) used as a pillory for those who infringed church rules. Notice the piece of Pictish sculptured stone at the foot of the tower.

Witches. Near the lochan just beyond the hilltop cairn on Castle Law is where local witches were supposed to have held their covens. The hill, Quarrel Knowe, legend tells, is where the witches met to settle their differences. Witches Road, again according to legend, is where women accused of being witches were led along for burning on Abernethy Hill (to your left) and where their ashes were scattered.

Walk 10

1. Return to the High Street and turn right to pass the post office. Walk right up narrow Kirk Wynd, where the Abernethy Glen Walk is signposted. Go past a striking church, which at the time of publication is undergoing reconstruction and is set to provide attractive living accommodation. Continue along a lane where, in autumn, the hedgerows are laden with hips, haws and blackberries.

2. Where the road divides take the left branch and go on to where it becomes a track. Follow it as it swings to the right. It passes below Loanhead Quarry, which was used for the production of road metal and chips before the seam ran out in 1942. Now its face is clad with heather and long grass, and trees grow about its top and on any ledge where roots can take hold. Pause on the seat to enjoy the view over the lower Earn valley and then walk on where the slopes to the left are steep and tree-clad. To the right are pastures and the town lies beyond.

3. Follow the path (Witches Road) into deciduous woodland. Below to your right, the Ballo Burn chuckles as it hurries through the trees. Descend rather steep steps to the side of the burn. Continue along the path beside the stream and where it begins to climb,

41

cross duckboards and pass through a gate. Turn right and walk a couple of steps to the road.

4. Turn right and follow the waymark, directing you along the road in the direction of Glenfoot. Look for the sign on the left for Castle Law. Follow the stony cart track uphill and go on where it swings left and then right, easing the gradient, to a signpost directing you along a path to the summit, from where there are grand views. An iron-age fort here dates from about 500 to 300 BC Just beyond is the small lochan which could have supplied the fort and the place where the witches are supposed to have met.

5. Return the same way and turn left to walk the road. Turn right, just after the small hill, Quarrel Knowe. Walk past large gates on your left, belonging to the water board, and continue along a rough track of chippings. It runs through the Rough Glen and was once part of a public road along which were carried great quantities of lime and coal. Climb a ladder stile and continue along the peaceful, tree-lined track.

6. Climb the next ladder-stile and from here look for stones in the track that were part of a highway before 1820. Step out along the reinforced track until you reach the road. Turn right and walk in front of Tootie House, where once the cowherd sounded his horn. He alerted people to release their cows so that they could be taken to the common grazing ground. Walk on to the small square with its memorial cross. Here look for the round tower on the left. From here it is just a short walk to the car park

Bramble and hips

Practicals

Type of walk: A delightful walk, with pleasing views, along rough ways through the hills behind Abernethy.

Distance:	3 miles
Time:	2 hours
Maps:	OS Landranger 58, Pathfinder 361
Terrain:	Some rough tracks but generally easy.

11

Kinnoull Hill, east of Perth

Cross the Tay by the northernmost bridge in Perth, from west to east, and drive ahead to climb uphill. Pass the hospital and continue until you see a signpost, directing you right, for Kinnoull Hill Forest Walks. Drive along the narrow road to park in the quarry car park, grid ref. 135235, where there is a map of the hill that gives suggestions for walks.

The summit. The summit cairn tells you that Lord Dewar gave this lovely hill to the city of Perth in 1923. The secondary summit cairn has a view indicator panel, helping you identify the wonderful panorama. Close by is a stone table, rather near to the edge of the sheer cliffs of the hill. From here you can enjoy a glorious view of the River Tay meandering gracefully through its fertile plain, on its way to the sea, and of the motorway bridge. The table was erected by an Earl of Kinnoull, a former proprietor of the hill. Look left from here to see Kinnoull Tower built by the ninth Earl of Kinnoull as a ruin, a fashion of the time, after he had seen the castles of the Rhine on his Grand Tour. Below the Tower you can see Kinfauns Castle, built in 1825 for the Earl of Moray.

Kinnoull Tower

Walk 11

1. Leave the quarry car park by sturdy wooden steps. These lead to a wide grassy track signed to 'Summit' which climbs steadily through pleasing deciduous woodland. Many small tracks lead off the main one but ignore these and head for the heights. The track ascends through birch, with a glorious carpet of heather and bilberry. Follow the track straight up the hill until it joins a larger track on which you bear right.

2. Follow the wide way as it swings to the right, to pass through more woodland, passing another 'Summit' sign on the way. The route rises steadily, then drops for a short distance before rising again, more steeply, through broom bushes. Ahead lies the trig. point, bench seats and the two view cairns.

3. Walk on from the summit to the secondary summit with the stone table, more bench seats, and wide views over the Tay valley.

4. Turn left and follow the path down through woodland with a glimpse of the tower through the trees. At the bottom of the short descent, follow the track round to the right and climb up to the tower with more views across the wide strath below.

5. To return, take the path which goes into the woods directly away from the cliff edge, signed 'Nature Walk'. The path rises slightly and then descends through beautiful mixed pine and deciduous woodland with rowan, hazel and birch. Follow the path through a small stand of thick conifer plantation to join a larger path.

6. Continue down hill through open pine then larch woodland to a path junction. Turn left following the sign to 'Quarry Car Park'. Cross a dry ditch and bear right on a clear path through the woods, with glimpses of open fields beyond. Where several path converge

bear right towards a group of houses. Follow the path outside the garden hedges to emerge on an open hillside with a viewpoint and picnic tables. Enjoy the wide views over the city of Perth, then take the left-most path down the hill to the road at the entrance to the quarry car park.

Bilberry

Practicals

Type of walk: A pleasing short walk with great rewards along the way and from the summit.

Distance:	2 miles
Time:	1 hour
Maps:	OS Landranger 58, Pathfinder 350

12

Deuchny Hill

Leave Perth as for walk 11, and instead of turning right for Kinnoull Hill, continue along the road to the Jubilee car park, grid ref. 145237.

Perth was once the capital of Scotland. It was first settled over 8,000 years ago, and succeeding waves of Roman centurions, Pictish people and Celtic missionaries established themselves here, enjoying the good climate and the fertile farmlands. It was an ideal defensive and trading location at the edge of the Highlands. The town's position on the navigable River Tay enabled it to become an important trading port and it has kept its busy harbour to the present day.

Path, Deuchny Hill

Walk 12

1. Leave the north end of the car park by the waymarked track. Climb steadily uphill, with tall beech trees to the right and, to the left, splendid views over farmland. In high summer wild raspberries and rose bushes laden with hips grow along the verge. Pass the gate by the small covered reservoir and take the waymarked left turn. Pause here to enjoy the fine view of Perth below.

2. Follow the attractive grassy track through mixed woodland. Before the path starts to climb, leave it and turn left, as directed by a waymark, to walk down to a deer fence. Cross the stile and follow the continuing path through scots pine to another stile. Beyond, turn immediately right to reach a farm gate. Once through, head across the pasture towards the oak trees.

3. On reaching the oaks, turn right and head down to a wooden bridge over a stream, which you cross. Press on along the oak-lined path that follows the stream. On reaching the pine forest, pass through a gate which gives access to a wide track—Coronation Road, once part of the route taken by the Kings of Scotland on their way to be crowned at Scone Palace.

4. Carry on until you reach a waymark. This directs you right and uphill. At the top turn left to follow another track that curves round the side of a wooded hill. Soon the trees cease on the left and you have a marvellous view of the rolling countryside which leads down to the River Tay.

5. Go on along the gently sloping track, which leads you back into woodland. Then it emerges again to offer a panoramic view of the Tay and Kinnoull Hill. Follow the track as it winds among gorse and broom, to a point near the summit of the hill. The way then descends steadily to go over a crossroads and on. Near the bottom of the slope, turn acute right to pass through a kissing gate. At the road, turn right into the car park.

Wild raspberries

Practicals

Type of walk This is a delightful forest walk, particularly once the wide forest roads have been left behind. Enjoy the spectacular views.

Distance: 4 ½ miles
Time: 2 hours
Maps   OS Landranger 58, Pathfinder 350

13

Standing Stone and Stone Circle on the moors above Fowlis Wester and on to Loch Meallbrodden

To park at grid ref. 930250, head north-east from Crieff to Gilmerton. Continue on the A85 to New Fowlis. Then turn left up through Fowlis Wester and Pitlandy and left again to the parking area.

Fowlis Wester. The village is very small. Almost all of it can be seen from the square. It is difficult to believe that in 1794 the population was over a thousand and the village had two butchers, several tailors and many shoemakers and smiths. There were shops and inns and numerous weavers and farmers. It is equally difficult to believe that the main route to Perth passed through the small gap between the church and the post office.

Standing stones and stone circle, Braes of Fowlis

Close by the square is the magnificent church of St Bean. St Bean was an 8th century Irish missionary, grandson of the King of Leinster. There has been a church on this site for more than a thousand years. The present church dates from the 13th century and is well worth a visit.

The square is dominated by a Pictish cross slab of weathered red sandstone dating from the eighth or ninth century. Look for carvings on the stone and an iron ring. The stone was used as a pillory and miscreants were chained to it and pelted with eggs.

Standing Stone and Stone Circle. The magnificent bronze age standing stone and the remains of the stone circle are seen on the moors above Fowlis Wester. Alas many of the stones of the circle were removed in the 19th century and used for house and wall building.

Walk 13

1. After closing the gate beyond the parking area, walk ahead along the track that crosses the moorland. In late August the way passes through a great mass of heather. Leave the track just before a derelict building and walk left to see the standing stone. Close by it are the remains of the stone circle. What a wonderful view our ancestors had from this ridge moor.

2. Continue along the track, where grouse feed on heather shoots, and follow it as it begins to descend gently. At the junction, take the right branch and continue along the right side of a conifer plantation. Cross a wide footbridge over a small stream and walk on. To the left lies little Loch Meallbrodden, a delightful expanse of water with deciduous trees to the right and a plantation of conifers beyond. The loch is the haunt of mallard and these alight and take off with much splashing.

3. Pass through the gate on the left in the fence, just before a huge ash. Walk ahead, keeping to the right of a farm barn. Stroll along the path, which keeps close to the loch. Climb the stile and walk on. Cross the loch's overflow, wading if necessary, to walk along the dam at its head. At the end of the dam, cross the wooden footbridge over Muckle Burn. Follow the lovely track as it swings left through firs, passing a boathouse on the your left.

4. Go through a gate to follow the track onto the open moor. Continue along the track to return to your parking place.

Mallard and kingcups

Practicals

Type of walk: A delightful quiet walk across seemingly remote moorland to a pretty loch.

Distance:	2 ½ miles
Time:	1 ½ hours
Maps:	OS Landranger 52 or 58, Pathfinder 349
Terrain:	Easy walking but expect plenty of mud after rain.

14

Ben Lawers, Loch Tay

Park at the Visitor Centre, grid ref. 609379, operated by the National Trust for Scotland (NT).

Ben Lawers (1214m/3984ft) is the highest mountain in Perthshire. Its summit and southern slopes are owned by the National Trust, which has preserved its famous arctic-alpine flora, for the benefit of the public and for scientific research.

This flora thrives on the mountain's unique soil, a soft, lime rich schist. The area has always been popular with botanists. It was 'discovered' in 1790 and was a mecca for alpine botanists, collectors and alpine gardeners. In more recent times the pressure has eased and now people like to take photographs of plants rather than pick them.

The 8,000 acre property—Ben Lawers—was bought by the Trust in 1950 using some of the Mountainous Country Fund much of which was bequeathed by Percy Unna (1878–1950). He was President of the Scottish Mountaineering Club and it was through his farsightedness and his generosity that the Trust was able obtain other mountain properties including Glencoe, Kintail, Goat Fell, Torridon and the Grey Mare's Tail (Moffat).

Meall Corranaich, Ben Lawers and Beinn Ghlas

Scottish Blackface Sheep. These were originally from the Borders and were brought into Perthshire about 1800. Some of the sheep stay on the hill ground all the winter and when it is snow-covered the animals have to scrape the snow away to find food. Although the Trust owns the ground some farms below the Trust's have the right to graze a certain number of sheep on the hill for nothing. Farmers' traditional grazing rights were maintained as a condition of the sale of the land.

1. Leave the car park by the signposted footpath. In the wetter areas look for a plethora of moisture-loving plants. Climb the stile in the deer and sheep fence. Continue along the well maintained path, enjoying fine views down to Loch Tay. Cross the Burn of Edramucky and climb steadily towards a gate in the fence.

Walk 14

2. From now on you will see the Scottish Blackface sheep grazing. Go on over level moorland and then scale several large steepish hummocks to reach the summit of Beinn Ghlas (1103m/3657ft. Beyond the path slopes gently down before continuing as an airy ridge walk between two corries. Head across a short shoulder, where to the right lies a small lochan.

53

3. Then begins the steep and fairly lengthy climb to the summit. The path, rocky and rough in places, is easy to follow—some scrambling is required over several more rocky humps. Look in spring on the rocks for purple saxifrage or, a little later, for moss campion. At the top stands a trig point and a cairn. The views from here are magnificent. You can spot the major peaks of Perthshire and sometimes the Atlantic and the North Sea.

4. Leave the summit and return to the small lochan. Here you may wish to retrace your outward route. This walk takes a path to the right off the ridge route, following it as it contours the side of Beinn Ghlas, passing below a corrie. Look back down Gleann Da-Eig, through which meanders the Allt Gleann Da-Eig, to Glen Lyon far below. The path, occasionally waymarked, passes easily through a tumble of boulders where fir club moss thrives. Then it joins an old track coming up from shielings in Gleann Da-Eig and crossing the col between Beinn Ghlas and Meall Corranaich. Continue down this and soon the Visitor Centre comes into view.

Purple saxifrage

5. On reaching your outward route just before the stile, turn right and walk downhill.

Practicals

Type of walk: This is an exciting walk but not one to be taken lightly. Care is needed and it should only be undertaken by those with walking boots, waterproofs and hill walking experience. Do not attempt in the mist and turn back if mist descends.

Distance: 7 miles
Time: 5–6 hours
Maps: OS Landranger 51, Pathfinders 322 and 335
Terrain: Some level moor and some rough rocky steep terrain.

15

Falls of Acharn

Leave your car in the parking area, grid ref. 756438, close to the signposted start of the walk.

Dorothy Wordsworth's comments, in 1803, on her visit to the Falls of Acharn are reported by Louis Stott in his book of Scottish waterfalls as follows:

> We entered a dungeon-like passage and, after walking some yards in total darkness found ourselves in a quaint apartment stuck over with moss, hung about with stuffed foxes and ornamented with a library of wooden books covered with old leather backs, the mock furniture of a hermit's cell. At the end of the room, through a large bow window, we saw the waterfall, and at the same time looking down to the left, the village of Kenmore and part of the lake—a very beautiful prospect.

The **Burn of Acharn** gathers its waters from a large area below Sron a' Chaoineidh. It then tumbles down a hanging valley to enter Loch Tay close to Acharn Point and west of Kenmore.

Falls of Acharn

The last glaciers retreated from these parts about 10,000 years ago leaving flat-bottomed, steep-sided, U-shaped valleys. The main valley of the Tay was deepened more than the smaller tributary valleys. Waterfalls are a feature of these hanging valleys where side streams, such as the Acharn, drop down steep slopes to reach the main valley.

Walk 15

1. From the parking area, head up the reinforced track. Look back often to see Loch Tay overlooked by Drummond Hill. To the west lies Ben Lawers. As you climb, the river is lost to sight deep in its gorge but the sound of its descent fills the air.

2. Follow the signpost for the Hermit's Cave, a folly, and walk through a dark tunnel to a railed platform for a wonderful view of the falls, where the burn descends over stepped ledges of flaggy Dalradian rocks. Then the raging water drops for many feet in a curtain of white lace, divided near its base by a projecting boulder. The resultant twin falls hurtle into a dark brown pool. Next, the water is imprisoned by the sides of a narrow ravine before raging into a second pool. From here it slides to the left at right angles to the main fall before it plummets deeper into the glen. Miss Wordsworth would have been more impressed if she could have stood out on the railed platform.

3. Return through the tunnel and turn left to continue. Follow the curving path around the top of the ravine beneath lofty beech. Here a signboard directs you left to a viewing area. This is a walkway and footbridge constructed from timber by Royal Engineers in 1989. It provides an excellent view of the upper falls. The racing burn tumbles over rocks, scouring out cavities and undermining the sides of the narrow gorge. While standing on the bridge, close to the walls of the gorge, look for the many ferns, mosses and lichens growing here.

4. Do not cross the bridge but return to the main track and continue up the to the High Bridge—a traditional stone structure giving a good view down the canyon scoured out by the churning waters. To descend go through a kissing gate and down the path on the right bank of the burn. After negotiating more of the sappers' wooden steps and bridgework, pause at a convenient seat on a rocky outcrop for a view across to the Hermit's Cave, with Ben Lawers in the background.

5. Continue downhill to the end of the track, where there is an old water-mill, now a private house. A few steps, left over the road bridge, take you back to your car.

Moss and liverwort

Practicals

Type of walk: A dramatic ascent and descent beside a raging burn along good footpaths, with exciting viewing platforms and walkways to obtain the best views.

Distance:	1 ½ miles
Time:	1 hour
Maps:	OS Landranger 51 or 52, Pathfinder 322
Terrain:	Easy underfoot as you climb and descend but strong footwear required.

16

The Birks of Aberfeldy and the Falls of Moness

Visitors to Aberfeldy are given every encouragement to explore the Birks (old Scots for birches) and the wonderful waterfalls on the Moness Burn. There are two free car parks off the A826 Aberfeldy—Crieff road, (clearly signposted on the right if coming from the centre of town). The top one, grid ref. 855485, is more convenient and has a dispenser offering a useful leaflet about the nature trail. In the unlikely event of the space being full, drive back a few metres to the lower park and walk back up.

Den. In the Scottish dialect 'den' means 'a wooded glen', an apt description for the Den of Moness.

Burns's seat

The Birks o' Aberfeldy. Below is an extract from a song by Robert Burns. The poet was inspired to write this after a visit to the Den of Moness on the 30 August, 1787. As a result the Den, with its Falls of Moness, has been maintained as a scenic walk for over 200 years. Burns is believed to have composed the song on a rocky ledge (known as Robert Burns's seat) at the side of the ravine, shaded by a rocky overhang and surrounded by trees and lush vegetation.

Bonnie lassie, will ye go,
Will ye go, will ye go;
Bonnie lassie, will ye go
To the birks of Aberfeldy?

Now simmer blinks on flowery braes,
And o'er the crystal streamlet plays;
Come, let us spread the lightsome days
In the birks of Aberfeldy.

While o'er their heads the hazels hing,
The little birdies blithely sing,
Or lightly flit on wanton wing
In the birks of Aberfeldy.

The braes ascend like lofty wa's,
The foaming steam deep-roaring fa's,
Overhung wi' fragrant spreading shaws
The birks of Aberfeldy.

Walk 16

Birch Trees. The birch is the most common tree to be found at the highest part of the walk. Birch produces vast quantities of small winged seeds which are easily dispersed by the wind. Where the ground has been disturbed the birch can colonise readily and is fast growing, taking advantage of the lack of competition.

1. Start the walk from the car park and, when the track divides, ignore the signs for the left fork. This is your return route. Go straight ahead, keeping to the west bank of the burn. The way passes beneath magnificent beech trees. Gradually the gorge deepens and you can no longer see the burn—only hear it raging on its way.

59

2. Continue on, climbing higher and higher, until the path passes beneath birch. Pause on a convenient seat before carrying on up the path. Cross a small bridge and take a long pause on the next seat from where there is a magnificent view of the Perthshire hills. The noise of the Moness increases but not a glimpse of the falls is yet seen. Peer over the protective fence at the sheer sides of the gorge. When you reach a fork, go down left to cross the bridge over the spectacular falls. Though they rage and roar, it is still difficult to see their full magnificence.

Wood vetch

3. From the bridge, climb again to continue up steps. Then begin your descent of a series of steps to a wonderful viewpoint, where the Falls of Moness can be seen in all their glory. The burn drops in three great white-topped falls, crashing over ledges and plunging into pools and a continual noise resounds from this dramatic hollow. Spray fills the air and covers the luxuriant vegetation. Birch, larch and scots pine line the sides of the gorge.

4. Follow the path as it zig-zags down, dropping rapidly, well stepped and railed. Look for the pretty wood vetch flourishing here. Continue ahead to another viewing point where the burn comes down in innumerable cascades before descending in one long jet into a very deep pool. The sides of the gorge flare upwards. The rock face beside the viewpoint is dripping with water and here liverworths thrive, together with the fragile feather, fork and hair mosses. In spring vast sheets of golden saxifrage brighten the ravine.

5. Return and continue your descent along a pleasingly constructed wooden walkway. Cross the next bridge, from where you can almost touch a graceful fall, on a tributary burn. Stroll along the path to see yet another side fall which rages down rocky ledges to join the Moness. Follow the path downwards to see the burn's final plummeting descent. Look for Robert Burns' seat as you walk on.

6. Carry on along the stepped way to pass yet another fall and then go on along another very satisfying wooden way, built by sappers in 1986. Finally you reach the bed of the ravine, with its tree-clad sides towering overhead. The path goes on over the Moness and returns you to the upper car park.

Silver birch

Practicals

Type of walk: A magical walk, particularly on the descent, to view another of Perthshire's many glorious waterfalls.

Distance:	2 miles
Time:	2 hours
Maps:	OS Landranger 52, Pathfinder 323
Terrain:	The path is rough in places and runs along steep slopes where young children should be kept in sight at all times. Sturdy footwear essential, particularly after wet weather.

17

A walk from Amulree round Loch Freuchie

Park in a layby with a disused hut, opposite the Amulree Hotel, grid ref. 901367.

Loch Freuchie or Fraoch—the heathery loch. The loch, a long stretch of silvery water, fills a quiet hollow in Glen Quaich. Half way down the loch is one small island covered with pines. This is a crannog, a prehistoric man-made island. Legend has it that a young lover, Fraoch, braved a dragon that dwelt there to obtain rowan berries for his lady, Maidh. He successfully completed his task having evaded the dragon. But Maidh insisted that she wanted the tree as well. So he returned but on uprooting it, disturbed the dragon. During the ensuing fight the dragon gnawed off Fraoch's limbs but he still managed to slay the beast. Maidh found both lying dead on the shore of the crannog.

Amulree Church

Amulree. The hamlet lies almost 1000ft/306m above sea level and is very close to the geographical centre of Scotland. The picturesque white-painted church was built in 1744. The Amulree Hotel started life in 1714 as a drovers' inn. It became a 'King's House' when General Wade was building his roads and the nearby bridge. After that it was a coaching inn.

Walk 17

1. Walk uphill past the picturesque church and the post office and general stores. Turn right to walk the narrow road to Kenmore. The way quickly moves out in the heather-clad hills. Look for your first glimpse of Loch Freuchie.

2. At the head of the loch, take the track on the right, signposted Amulree. Cross the pretty bridge over the River Quaich just before it adds its water to the loch. Here anglers fish for pike and picnickers enjoy the grassy banks. Follow the track through the buildings of Turrerich to pass through a gate. Beyond, a signpost points the direction for Amulree.

3. Cross a tractor bridge over a stream and step out along the track, which runs well above the shore of the loch. Notice as you go the ruined settlements, close to small streams, strung out along this sunny south-west facing bank of the loch. In 1746 more than a thousand inhabitants were of an age to study their catechism. By

the 1800s more than 300 crofters had left the glen to resettle in Canada, where they named their settlements Amulree and Glenquaich.

4. The gated track passes into a large area of birch woodland. Continue past the foot of the loch and go on by two plantations of conifers. At the branching of the track, take the right fork to walk in front of Lochan Lodge and then to the road. Turn right and cross the two-arched bridge over the River Braan, and carry on to the layby.

Pike lurking

Practicals

Type of walk: A pleasing fairly level walk along a quiet minor road, returning beside a charming loch.

Distance:	8 miles
Time:	4–5 hours
Maps:	OS Landranger 52, Pathfinder 336

18

Dunkeld, Lowes Nature Reserve, the Hermitage and Rumbling Bridge, by the River Braan

The Hermitage (Ossian's Hall) Dunkeld

I. Park in the lovely town of Dunkeld, grid ref. 025426, and walk from here through Cathedral Street, past houses well restored by the National Trust and Perth County Council. Go through the huge wrought-iron gates of the cathedral. To the left lawns, with scattered trees, slope gently to the banks of the wide, stately Tay. To the right lies the ruined cathedral.

The Cathedral. It took nearly 200 years to complete (1312–1501). In 1560, after the Reformation, it was largely destroyed. Today the restored choir area serves as the parish church. Enjoy the peace to be found within. Look for the 9th century Pictish Apostles' Stone on the right as you enter the Chapter House museum. Behind the carved oak screen, see the recumbent figure of Alexander Stewart, Earl of Badenoch, who lived at Garth Castle—see walk 24. Read the page from the Book of Ruth in the Great 'She ' Bible printed in 1611.

II. Park at the Loch of Lowes Nature Reserve, grid ref. 041436, and then pass through the Visitor Centre to two bird hides.

Ospreys. Use the binoculars and telescopes provided to view the ospreys in their nests atop the pines. The adult birds make excursions to the loch to fish and bathe. Look for tufted duck, great crested grebe, coot, pochard and goosander idling on the lovely stretch of water.

III. Park in the lower car park, grid ref. 013423, for the National Trust's Hermitage Woodland Walk.

The Hermitage is a beautiful wooded area of 37 acres alongside the River Braan, which here descends in several waterfalls, rapids and cascades. The woodland was created in the 18th century by the Dukes of Atholl as a wild tree garden.

Walk 18

1. Buy a leaflet at the start to enhance your walk. Leave the parking area by the waymarked route behind the board, which gives information about the Hermitage. At waymark 3 you pass below a stand of enormous Douglas fir. At waymark 5 you continue beneath silver fir to a wooden fence. From here look across the river, dark and brooding, to what is reputed to be the tallest tree in Britain, a Douglas fir well over 62m/200ft.

2. Cross the 18th century bridge, spanning a narrow gorge where the River Braan cuts through a rocky ravine below the Black Linn fall. Continue along the woodland way that leads off left on the far side of the river. It climbs high above the hurrying burn. Look back for a grand view of the waterfall bridge. Press on until you reach a gate on to the road. Here if you wish you can head downhill to Inver and along the A9 for a very short distance back to the car park.

3. To continue with this walk, retrace your steps to the bridge and cross. Enter the Hermitage Folly or Ossian's Hall, built in 1758 by the future third Duke of Atholl. From the balcony there is a dramatic view of the falls. Walk further along the waymarked trail. Just beyond waymark 10, look for Ossian's Cave which, like the Hermitage, is a romantic folly. Beyond the cave follow the narrow path through the trees, still within sound of the burn. At the next waymark, continue ahead to walk through more conifer woodland. Follow the path as it swings to the left and climbs uphill.

67

4. Continue in the direction of the signposted Rumbling Bridge. Cross a wooden footbridge to pass through a kissing gate. Walk the wide grassy track over open pasture. After the next kissing gate, turn left and walk downhill to the famous bridge. Here the Braan rages through a rocky canyon far below the single-span bridge. As it surges beneath a great overhang, the noise echoes or rumbles as if from an enormous underground cavern. It is an impressive place.

5. Return to the signpost on the edge of the forest. Continue ahead to a forest road and walk downhill.

6. Look for the signpost to the Hermitage. Follow the directions to the right into the trees then bear left to follow the waymarks leading back to the car park.

Practicals

Type of walk: This charming walk takes you through magnificent woodland about the River Braan. It visits two romantic 18th century follies and crosses a fine bridge where the Braan is at its most impressive.

Distance: 5 miles
Time: 2 ½ hours
Maps: OS Landranger 52, Pathfinder 324

Red deer

Glen Garr And Craig Obney

Leave the A9, close to Dunkeld, by the A822 in the direction of Crieff. After two miles, look for a turn on the right signposted Rumbling Bridge. Go down the lane and use one of the ample parking areas on the right, grid ref. 997412.

Cairns—remains of old fort, Craig Obney

Rumbling Bridge. If you have time to spare and have not already seen the sight (it forms the climax of walk 18, approached from the H e r m i t a g e , downstream) it is well worth the few minutes it takes to follow the track to the bridge and look into the dramatic chasm, with the waters of the River Braan crashing noisily below.

1. From the parking area follow the instructions for the start of the Braan Walk, which initially takes the same route as the Glen Garr walk. The way takes you through oak woodland and across a footbridge. Beyond, turn right to reach the A822, which you cross to walk on up the wide farm track opposite, signposted Glen Garr. Just before the second cattle grid a track leads left for Tomgarrow, which you ignore. Continue climbing gently. Look left to see a lochan sparkling in the sunshine. This is where the Inchewan Burn, seen on walk 20, originates. Ahead lies Birnam Hill, with the cairn on King's Seat, perched on its heather-clad mound, seen on the same walk.

2. Cross another cattle grid and walk ahead to take a signposted grassy track for Glen Garr and Bankfoot, continuing between derelict

walls. Then, where the track winds off left to Balhomish farm, climb the stile and go on over pasture. Here you might hear curlews call and then see them take flight. Beyond the next two stiles the track leads into glorious heather moorland.

3. Walk the path as it moves into a wetter area, where bog rosemary grows, and cross two small streams on conveniently placed stones. Pass beneath a solitary pine. Away to the right stands Craig Gibbon, topped with scots pine. The path climbs steadily through mixed bracken and heather. Birches dot the hillside on the lower slopes of the Obney Hills, which lie to the left.

4. Stride along the lovely high-level path. Soon after passing a clump of birch on the right, look out for a narrow path to the right leading, after a few steps, to a promontory overlooking the steep-sided glen. From this fine viewpoint Glen Garr opens up beneath you, with the Garry Burn winding down through the trees. The clear remains of an old light railway track can be seen leading ahead, straight down the valley below the spoil heaps of a now defunct quarry, which it once served. The quarry took slate from the steep rocky side of Craig Gibbon, now straight across from where you stand.

5. Return to the main track and at this point a decision must be made whether to continue down the pleasantly graded route to where it ends at Upper Obney farm and then returning to Rumbling Bridge the way you came. Or, to take a more strenuous circuit, climbing the steep slope ahead of you to the summit of Craig Obney, with its prehistoric fort and wonderful views. If the latter is your choice then this is the way this walk continues.

6. On returning to the main track from the Glen Garr viewpoint, go straight across the track and up the slope passing through mixed bracken and heather. There are faint traces of a path but this peters out as you reach solid heather up the slope. Make your way over to the right towards higher ground through the boot tangling sweetly perfumed plant. Deer trods and slate outcrops make the going marginally easier. Continue on steadily climbing to the trig point. Pause on the pleasing summit, with its well proportioned cairn, and survey the fascinating circle of stones forming the outline of an ancient fort. Enjoy the glorious views. In the foreground to the west, look for the obelisk on the summit of Craig Gibbon, circled by pines. This structure is marked on the map, but it was obscured by trees when walking the glen path below.

7. The descent uses an estate track serving shooting butts. Once it led to a quarry whose remains, if you walk over to the eastern ramparts of the fort, are clearly to be seen on the hillside below. This track is your descent route and it can be seen starting on the broad col to the left of the quarry. Head towards this by going steadily down through the heather on your left. Go carefully down the hillside, which is at first steep, with rocky outcrops. Some of the deer trods are useful, providing relief from walking on the springy heather tufts. There is a good chance of seeing a group of red deer leaping away as you head for the track.

8. When you reach the track, turn left and follow it for a mile and a half until it swings left and ends abruptly at a farm gate. Here go down left by the fence, cross the boggy burn and climb up to a gate by an old sheepfold, which you passed on your outward walk.

9. Turn right over the stile and return to the parking area by following your outward route.

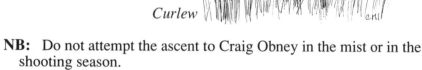

Curlew

NB: Do not attempt the ascent to Craig Obney in the mist or in the shooting season.

Practicals

Type of walk: A very pleasing walk, with some exciting scrambling up to the trig point on Craig Obney. Enjoy all the magnificent views as you go

Distance: 8 miles
Time: 4–5 hours
Maps: OS Landranger 52 or 53, Pathfinders 324 and 337

20

Birnam Hill

To park, leave the A9 at the A923 turn-off for Dunkeld. In a few yards turn right for Birnam and park in a large layby, grid ref. 032418, on the right side of the road.

Birnam Hill The steepish climb to the summit is rewarded by superb views over the Perthshire Highlands and southwards towards the fertile lowland plains. The hill is famed for its Shakespearean associations; it was here that King Duncan's son Malcolm is reputed to have made camp before marching to Dunsinane to defeat Macbeth.

The famous Birnam Oak is said to be the last relic of ancient Birnam Wood. The surrounding hills support fine woodland, much of it carefully planted during the last two centuries by the Dukes of Atholl and, more recently, by the Forestry Commission.

Birnam is the sister community of Dunkeld, with the two settlements linked by Telford's Bridge over the Tay. The seven-arched bridge was built in 1809, and its toll-

Stair bridge

house can still be seen. The village owes its existence largely to the 19th century railway builders who sited Dunkeld Station on the south bank of the Tay. It was built here, in 1856, because the 6th Duke of Atholl refused to let the railway cross his estates. It took another seven years for the Duke to agree to the railway continuing over his land on its way to Inverness. During this time English families rented villas in Birnam—among them was Beatrix Potter's family.

Walk 20

1. Walk past the public toilets on the opposite side of the road. Turn right and walk on along Birnam Glen, signposted Birnam Hill Walk. Pass under the A9 and the bridge carrying the Perth to Inverness railway. Use the footpath on the left to continue uphill. Look through the trees for the pretty waterfall on the Inchewan Burn. Follow the signpost for the Birnam Hill Walk and King's Seat, crossing a narrow road and walking uphill along a leafy track.

2. At a junction where there is a 'Private—No Entry' sign, bear right and then left, following the Inchewan Burn. Soon a waymark directs you left and steeply uphill through silver birch, oak and willow, with wood sage and bracken beneath. A strategically placed seat

gives you a chance to get your breath. Continue climbing, with many a stop to look back at the pleasing views. Look for the Telford Bridge over the Tay, and then the three lochs north-east of Dunkeld. Soon the bracken is left behind and you move into heather, cowberry and bilberry.

3. Follow the clear path to climb onto a craggy viewpoint (306m/1000ft) and here you will want to linger. Stride on over the heather-clad crown where you might see red deer race between larches. Keep to the path, ahead, as you cross a wet patch and then, in the centre of a vast area of heather, rears a large mound. This is King's Seat (404m/1333ft) and from its summit the whole of Perthshire seems to lie at your feet.

4. A waymark directs you off the summit. Climb the next slope where a little scrambling is required. Now below you can see the A9 winding into the distance. Below too, stands picturesque Rohallion Lodge, with its conical turrets, sitting beside an artificial lake. Begin the steeply stepped descent, and follow the waymark at the bottom, which directs you right. Keep to the path and continue where it becomes a track. Alpine club moss grows about the way.

5. Stride the now-grassy track, which has more waymarks to keep you safely on the route. It swings left and begins to drop down and down into a birch glade. Turn right at the arrow and signboard for Stair Bridge, passing through birch and rowan. To the left, look for the battlemented start of the bridge. Drop down the narrow path and cross a small stream, Birnam Burn, to see the splendid single-arched bridge high above you. Return from the stream to stand on the bridge and enjoy the fine views of woodland and several small lochs. Retrace your steps to the signpost for Stair Bridge.

Alpine clubmoss

6. Continue on, passing a stone seat. Head along the path to take the well signposted left turn for Rohallion Castle, the remains of an old tower. Some effort has been made to reconstruct the building. It is in a hidden hollow with a good view over the countryside below.

7. Head back to the main path and carry on downhill. To visit King's Rock continue along the track, passing through a high gate. Ignore the right turn to Rohallion Lodge and stride along the easy-to-walk ride in the direction of Birnam Wood. This takes you to the grand viewpoint.

8. Walk back along the track to the high gate. Turn right to follow a narrow path that drops steadily through magnificent birch woodland that masks Birnam Quarry. At the bottom of the long trail, turn right and walk to the gate before a railway bridge. Pass to the right of the gate and walk below the bridge.

9. Turn left to walk along the B867, Bankfoot Road. At the A9, cross, with care, and walk left in the direction of Inverness. In 46m/50yds turn right to take the old road leading into Birnam. After another 92m/100yds, look for the stile signposted Birnam circular walk. Stroll the metalled road and continue along the track beyond. Waymarks direct you to the riverside walk beside the fast-flowing River Tay. Walk this lovely path beneath enormous beeches and oaks. Continue past a children's park and then turn left just before the Birnam Oak. The track leads to the main street of Birnam. Turn right to regain your car.

Practicals

Type of walk: A steep hill walk taking your through mixed woodland, over heathery moorland, past a ruined castle, by a fascinating bridge and returning beside the River Tay.

Distance:	7 miles
Time:	4 hours
Maps:	OS Landranger 52, Pathfinders 324 and 337

21

River Ericht, Blairgowrie

Park in the Mill Inch free car park, grid ref. 180453, which is signposted down a narrow lane on the north side of Wellmeadow Green at the centre of Blairgowrie.

Cargill's Leap. This is now seen from a viewing platform erected by the local council. From here you look down on the racing river, which is divided by huge boulders into two streams. The smaller stream flows through a narrow deep chasm that confines the roaring water. The main stream passes down an even narrower canyon and rages and foams in fury at its fetters. And then both streams unite to fall into a large deep pool where salmon leap. This part of the

Cargill's Leap

river is known as Cargill's Leap—named after a local man who in 1681 leapt across the narrow chasm to escape his pursuers.

Raspberries And Jute. This part of Perthshire, with its sandstone loam, is the centre of the soft fruit industry that is restoring the prosperity first brought by the jute mills.

Walk 21

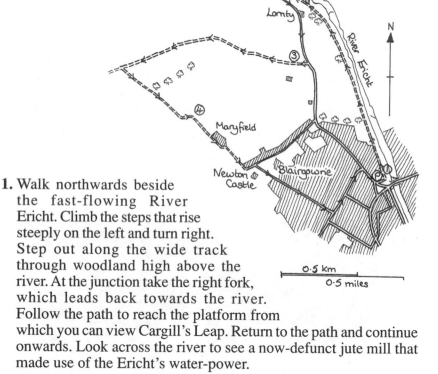

1. Walk northwards beside the fast-flowing River Ericht. Climb the steps that rise steeply on the left and turn right. Step out along the wide track through woodland high above the river. At the junction take the right fork, which leads back towards the river. Follow the path to reach the platform from which you can view Cargill's Leap. Return to the path and continue onwards. Look across the river to see a now-defunct jute mill that made use of the Ericht's water-power.

2. Bear right to stand on a footbridge that gives you a grand view of the river and of a spectacular weir upstream Walk back to the path and on past another mill. Look for its water-wheel hidden deep in the vegetation. Pass two cottages and then Brooklinn Mill, and beyond look for another weir over which slides a lace-like curtain of water. Press on to a narrow metalled road. Here turn left and climb the tree-lined way past Lornty farm to the top.

3. Turn right into an un-made road and walk uphill, with acres of raspberries growing on either side. Carry on uphill and then 180m/200yds before the reinforced track turns sharp right, look for a kissing gate on the left almost hidden by vegetation. Beyond the gate follow the path which stretches ahead between two enormous fields. Look for tiny white pansies and red hemp nettle growing in the rough grass edging the path. Pass through a kissing gate at its end and sit on the seat beyond. Enjoy the view, using the indicator set on a boulder, next to the seat, that describes the valley below and the hills beyond.

4. Follow the wide track that drops downhill. The way passes Maryfield farm under a row of lofty poplars, and on to Newton Road. Turn right to walk past Newton Castle. At the end of the road, turn left into Perth Street and follow it round until you reach the lane going down to the car park.

Pansies, trefoil, thyme

Practicals

Type of walk: This is a most enjoyable easy walk along a lovely river and returning through fields.

Distance:	4 miles
Time:	2 ½ hours
Maps:	OS Landranger 53, Pathfinder 324

22

Den of Alyth and the Hill of Alyth

Take the minor road which leaves Alyth Square on the south side and continue past the church, on the right, and the Alyth Burn on the left. This is the road to Bamff, and shortly after passing the de-restriction sign the Den of Alyth car park is signposted on the left, grid ref. 235487.

Den. The Den, the deep-sided wooded valley of the Alyth Burn, is designated a site of special scientific interest. The steep cliffs and the bouldery bed of the Alyth burn were shaped by glaciers moving south from the main Cairngorm ice mass. The valley has been wooded for several thousand years. The steep sides of the

Path, Den of Alyth

Den have probably protected the woods by making the removal of timber difficult.

Alyth is a farming town. Throughout the centuries it has managed to avoid destruction. It once earned its living by jute milling and weaving. Local layered and jointed sandstone, quarried nearby, was used to build Alyth as it expanded rapidly in the 1800s.

Walk 22

1. Start down the steps towards the picnic and children's play area, then turn to walk upstream. Stroll the path beneath alder, sycamore, oak, hazel and ash. Where the way branches, take the left fork, to continue below the huge Old Red Sandstone cliffs, shadowing the dancing Alyth Burn. The rock face is covered with lichens, mosses, ferns and small trees that precariously find a foothold. Walk on through a clearing and then beneath some magnificent beech to a footbridge, which you cross.

2. Follow the path to the right and climb the steep slope, the way littered with beech mast. The river flows far below to the right. Descend the slope and follow the path which leads to an attractive stone bridge, built in 1914. Cross and turn left to continue along a path through trees, with the river to the left. Follow the path as it swings right and comes to a road.

3. Turn left to stride the shady road to a junction. Take the right branch,

Gorse

81

signposted Glenisla. Walk uphill, with a conifer plantation to the right. Beyond the woodland, in summer, the right side of this minor road is bordered with great clumps of gorse and spiked with foxgloves. Carry on until you reach a signpost for the Hill of Alyth.

4. A path climbs right, up the gorse-covered slope, which is overrun by rabbits. Follow the path as it swings left then right to join a wider track. Climb steadily to the left, keeping an extensive bank of gorse to your left, as you make for the highest point ahead. Suddenly you come upon a delightful lochan nestling in the fold of the hill-top.

Rabbit

5. Once over the top of the hill, aim for a track (an old drove road) beside a wire fence that runs downhill to a clump of scots pines. Beneath these is a kissing gate, which gives access to a fenced track. Enjoy the gentle walk downhill. Pass through another kissing gate, turn left and then almost immediately right down another track.

6. When you have passed the farmyard on your right, turn right into Strathmore Terrace and follow the road along which you drove earlier. The car park is a short distance along on the left.

Practicals

Type of walk: A delightfully easy walk of five miles passing through glorious woodland, beside a pleasing burn and over a hilltop with a splendid view.

Distance: 5 miles
Time: 3 hours
Maps: OS Landranger 53, Pathfinder 325

23

Carn Gorm/Carn Mairg Horseshoe

Park at Invervar, grid ref. 666483. To reach this look for a private track, signposted Inverinain and Dericambus, on the south side of the minor road from Fortingall to Bridge of Balgie. There is a parking area, on the right, a few yards down the track.

Ptarmigan are mountain grouse. They breed and live all year on the high tops. In winter their plumage is all white and provides perfect camouflage. In spring, after moulting, their bodies are grey with white feathered bellies and white under the wings. They feed on the shrubby heath vegetation found at high altitudes. When disturbed they scuttle away among the rocks, flying off only if in imminent danger. The live in families during the summer and congregate in large parties over the winter. Listen for their hoarse cackles as they take off when disturbed. When they land they begin to call again making quiet motorbike noises.

Invervar. This was once a thriving village with a school, shop, tailor, carpenter, weaver and a lint mill. Today little remains; the old mill, a small round building with a conical roof, sits in an idyllic woodland hollow beside a glacial mound with a leat from the burn running downhill.

*Ben Lawers and Beinn Ghlas
from Carn Gorm*

1. Return to the road, cross and go through the gate on the left of a stone building opposite. There is a large notice on gate giving details of access. Walk up the track past some cottages on the left. Cross left to see the remains of the lint mill. Follow the way as it crosses an open field, then winds up through a conifer wood. Emerge from the trees by a gate onto open fell. Continue on an excellent track, with the lovely Invervar Burn foaming below to your left.

2. Cross a side burn, the Allt Coire a' Chearcaill, on a stout bridge. Just before the next tributary joins the Invervar the deer fence, which has been beside you, turns away left and there is a rickety footbridge over the Invervar Burn. Cross this and follow a good 'walkers' path along the river bank to the end of the plantation. Here the path ascends the river terrace, scree covered and eroded. Aim for the small ruin above.

3. Beyond, go on the generally clear path leading up onto the spur of Carn Gorm, a shoulder below the summit, where the ground is stony. The summit (1029m/3014ft) has a cairn and is higher than the point to the north where the trig point lies on its side and is surrounded by a low wall. In mid-summer the schist is covered with clumps of moss campion and alpine ladies' mantle. The grass is spangled with mountain pansies.

4. Take the obvious path that leads quite steeply down to the north, to a col below the small top of An Sgorr. There are two ancient fence posts and the base of a wall and the path follows this to the top of the hill. Descend north to the next col and then climb gently, north-east, towards Meall Garbh (968m/3171ft). At the shoulder half way up a line of old rusty fence posts appears, and these can be followed to the top. Meall Garbh has two rocky summits of similar height— the north-west one, situated on the fence line is slightly higher and is adorned with a stone and fence post sculpture for a cairn.

5. Descend easily, north east to the next col, passing a small lochan— a likely place for spotting ptarmigan. Follow the fence over the col and east up the long gradual ascent towards Meall a' Bharr (1004m/3313ft). On reaching the ridge turn south-east and continue to the summit cairn on a small rocky outcrop.

6. Turn east again still keeping with the fence and continue along the ridge, descending slightly. The path then diverges from the fence and follows easier ground to the south. It then rises to the summit of Carn Mairg (1042m/3436ft) with its well built substantial cairn. Descend south east following a steepish path down through a boulder field. From the bottom of this a clear path contours round above the corrie of Gleann Pollaidh to the col between this and Gleann Muiliinn where you might stumble on families of golden plovers.

7. Follow the path over the col and onto Creag Mhor (981m/3213ft)—it becomes slightly indistinct higher up but the going is good. There are two summits and you arrive between them. The east one is the higher and consists of a pleasant little rocky tor. It's a good windbreak and you can sit here for your tea break and look over towards Schiehallion. A clear path take you along the top to the west summit with a superb view down onto Glen Lyon, with the river shining in the sunlight. Beyond lies the Lawers range, dark and imposing.

8. Return towards the col but before reaching it, drop down over grass, winding towards a path seen below. This heads off to the west down a long ridge and is a lovely way to descend—easily angled and mostly good underfoot, with fine views of the Lawers Hills and Glen Lyon. Towards the foot of the ridge a stalker's path crosses the walker's path. Continue on along the ridge on the walker's path and descend with it to join your outward route just above the point at which it leaves the wood. Retrace your steps from here to your car.

Ptarmigan

NB: Restrictions on access are given on the gate. No access in the stalking season. No dogs are allowed. You are asked to walk the route in the direction given in the guide above and to stay on the route. You are asked not to come down any other corries or ridges. The notice ends by saying that if the gate is locked please go and climb Ben Lawers. The gate is generally closed.

Practicals

Type of walk: This is a superb walk with magnificent views through a quiet unspoiled area. It is a big walk and tiring, though generally easy and straight forward. In mist the fence along the top is a good guide, but it is foolish to go up in uncertain weather without some prior experience of navigation. The ridges are big and not always well defined and a walker, in bad weather, could end up in quite the wrong place. On a long summer's day you will want to go on and on over the tops.

Distance: 10–11 miles
Time: 7 hours
Maps: OS Landranger 51, Pathfinders 308 and 322

24

Garth Castle

Park in the village of Keltneyburn, beside the monument to David Stewart, grid ref. 775492.

David Stewart. On merit alone he rose from the ranks to become a major general of the Black Watch. When all the records of the regiment were lost he rewrote them from the notes he had kept. They were published in 1822 and earned him the title of Historian of the Highlands.

Garth Castle. The castle, a square keep 18m/60ft high, stands on a promontory 8m/50ft above the confluence of Keltney Burn and Allt Coire Pheiginn. Here lived the notorious Alexander Stewart who disposed of his prisoners by pushing them from the top of the keep into the gorge below. His descendants lived here for many years and then the castle lay empty for many more. Some time in the 1950s it was restored by John Fry of the chocolate family. Now it is a private house.

Garth Castle

The map labels: B846, Inchgarth, Garth Castle, Waterfall, (2), Litigan, Waterfall, (3), Falls of Keltney, (4), B846, Coshieville, Mon, (P), Keltneyburn, N

Walk 24

0·5 km
0·5 miles

1. From the monument walk uphill along the reinforced track on the left. Continue where it swings to the left still climbing. Pass the Scottish Wildlife Trust Keltneyburn Reserve board and follow the track as it moves into birch woodland, its floor in spring white with wood sorrel,

with the noise of the burn very close. Where the track divides take the right branch, signposted Inchgarth. Ignore the left branch to Litigan. The way now keeps very close to the burn, which descends in innumerable white-topped falls.

2. Stride on along the track as it rises high above the burn—out of sight but still raging. In summer greater bellflower grows along the lush verges of the track. Where the track branches again, take the left fork for Garth Castle, and continue climbing beneath beech until you have an exciting view of the edifice.

3. Retrace your steps and head down for a closer look at the Falls of Keltney, which you will have

Greater bellflower

heard crashing down the glen during your ascent. The upper falls can be seen swirling through the rocks as you reach the gate and cattle grid just before the track comes down from Litigan. Here there is a grassy area on the left with a fence topped with barbed wire. Where this ends look for a stile which you cross. A short distance further enables you to see the main falls through the trees. It is not advisable to attempt to cross the next fence for a closer look.

4. Leave the fenced off area by another stile and rejoin the main track through a gate in the wall. A short distance down the track you can rejoin your car.

Tormentil

Practicals

Type of walk: A delightful short walk up the glen of the Keltneyburn to see a dramatic castle. At the entrance to the glen you can see evidence of 19th century industrialisation. Across the road from the parking area is the mill once used as a meal mill and also for producing cloth. Next to it is a working forge, once a thriving smithy. Close by are cottages which once housed mill workers. At Coshieville, just a little east, up the road, is a hotel which once accommodated the officers of troops who built General Wade's military road.

Distance:	2 ½ miles
Time:	1 hour
Maps:	OS Landranger 52, Explorer 21

25

Schiehallion

Park in the car park at Braes of Foss, grid ref. 752557.

Schiehallion means 'The fairy place of the Caledonians'. At 1083m/3547ft, it is considered Scotland's most perfect mountain due to its symmetrical cone shape—it is what everyone thinks a mountain should look like. In 1774 an expedition led by the Reverend Nevil Maskelyne, the Astronomer Royal, found its shape ideal for experiments to find the weight of the earth. One of the members of the expedition was a Charles Hutton, who first thought of using contour lines, now universally used on today's maps.

John Muir (1838–1914) was a conservationist and a visionary and one of the first persons to call for the conservation of wild

Schiehallion from River Tummel

places for their own sake. The John Muir Trust was founded in Scotland in 1983, to conserve the remaining wild places for people and for nature. The Trust owns nearly 45,000 acres in the Scottish highlands and islands. At the time of this book going to press it is appealing for funds to restore the popular path from the Braes of Foss to the summit of Schiehallion and for future management of this lovely mountain.

Walk 25

1. Walk to the end of the parking area and follow the narrow path to a stile. Beyond, cross a bridge over a small stream bordered with bog myrtle. Follow the clear, easy-to-walk path over pasture where, in summer, it is colourful with wild flowers. To the left lies a large stand of conifers.

2. Climb the next stile, with its interesting dog gate, and stride out into moorland, which in late summer is a pink haze with heather. Ignore the cart track that bisects the path and continue on aiming for the mountain ahead.

3. The path begins to climb, first gradually and then more steeply, to where the heather competes with cloudberry and alpine lady's mantle. Follow the path over a long stretch of peat where you climb more steadily. The way continues behind the hill that has been in view all the way from the car park and everyone thinks is the summit. Bear to the left, following the indistinct but well cairned route.

4. The peaty, grassy sward soon gives way to scattered boulders. Then begins the long climb over large boulders of quartz, all the way to the summit. Here the path is not clear underfoot but large cairns, strategically placed, lead you up the easiest way. It is exhilarating to step from boulder to boulder, gradually nearing the summit, but requires considerable concentration and nimbleness. The great reward is the magnificent view of Perthshire's other peaks and more.

5. To return, retrace your outward route.

Cloudberry

Practicals

Type of walk: This is a very good climb but walking boots, waterproofs, a map and compass are essential and care should be taken when stepping from boulder to boulder. Do not attempt in the mist.

Distance: 6 miles
Time: 5 hours
Maps: OS Landranger 52, Explorer 21, Pathfinder 308

26

River Tummel, Kinloch Rannoch

Park in the pleasing paved square of Kinloch Rannoch, grid ref. 662587, which is overlooked by the church of All Saints and the Dunalastair Hotel.

Loch Rannoch is magnificent—a long, narrow, deep ribbon of water, hemmed in by steep hillsides. At the western end lies the lonely Rannoch Moor. Only the railway line traverses this vast and empty wilderness engineered in such a way as to float on the great mosses that it crosses.

Black Wood of Rannoch. Along the south shore of Loch Rannoch thrive scots pine in extensive remnants of the ancient Caledonian Forest. Remnant pinewoods are characterised by pine trees of varying age with willow, birch and juniper scattered throughout. Here you might find flowering, at the right time of the year, orchids and wintergreen.

Falls of Alt Mor, Kinloch Rannoch

Walk 26

1. Walk north-east along the B846 until you reach J Brown's garage. Turn right into Allt Mor Crescent and bear right again beyond the chapel, following the way signposted Riverside Walk. Turn left to cross a footbridge over the Allt Mor and follow the path through deciduous trees. Where the track swings left to give access to dwellings, continue ahead along a signposted narrow path. Look left from here to see Craig Varr towering over mixed woodland. Stride along the path below birch. To the right the wide, fast flowing River Tummel races to join Dunalastair Water. The path comes to the small parking area by the river. From here there is a magnificent view of Schiehalllion framed by birch and scots pine.

2. Cross the road and pass through the gate following the signpost for Hillside Path. Walk beneath beech and sycamore. Almost immediately, strike left up what has recently become a forestry approach road. This wide track climbs parallel with the road below. When it makes a turn to the right, leave it by the original Hillside Path which goes down to the left through a gate and crosses a footbridge over a small burn. The path comes close to the road, then steps lead you upwards. It descends again gradually to the road by the Kinloch Rannoch Outdoor Centre.

3. Cross the road bridge over the Allt Mor, with its dramatic waterfall plunging down from the hill above, over huge slabs.

4. For the second part of the walk, go up the hill before Brown's garage to a notice board indicating the walks about the village, where the youth project responsible has laid out an attractive wildlife garden. Go through the gate ahead to a signpost indicating routes up to Craig Varr and along to Loch Rannoch. Follow the Loch Rannoch route, a level grassy path above a wall with fine views over the loch and across to Schiehallion and the lesser hills around it.

94

Rowan

5. At the gate leading on to the road, turn left back towards the village, and, at the first building on the right follow a signpost for the Riverside walk. Go through a tubular steel gate then the path bears left to another similar gate. Ahead, you come to a picnic area by the Loch Rannoch weir, with another informative notice board, explaining the functions of the lochs and rivers contributing to the Tummel Hydro-Electric system.

6. Carry on under the road bridge, turn left through a gate and go round the public toilets to regain the road by the square where you have parked.

Practicals

Type of walk: A delightful stroll beside a lovely river and through quiet woodland. Enjoy the dramatic views as you go.

Distance: 2 miles
Time: 1 hour
Maps: OS Landranger 42 or 51, Pathfinder 308

27

Allean Forest and Loch Bhac

Park in the Queen's View Centre by Loch Tummel, grid ref. 864598.

Queen's View. Before you start the walk, visit the viewpoint from which Queen Victoria viewed Loch Tummel and Schiehallion, the well-shaped mountain at the head of the loch. Though the weather was fine for her and the view good the Queen records in her diary not her thoughts about the view but about the poor cup of tea brewed on her picnic We can all appreciate her feelings.

Loch Bhac

The Clachan is a typical 18th century farm settlement, parts of which have been reconstructed. Notice the cornkiln on the right, later used as a limekiln. Beyond stands a ruin that was possibly a milking byre. On the left of the track lies a house and an animal house. Both have been restored and have splendid turf roofs.

1. Leave the visitor centre and walk up the road to the left for a few steps. When you reach the road sign telling drivers coming from the west that they will reach the visitor centre in 100yds, take a faint path that leads up the slope on the right. After a dozen steps the path becomes a wide grassy track that swings left through the trees, rising steadily. At the junction turn left and continue along the track. This joins a major forest track coming up from the left. Bear right up this.

2. The wide forest track passes through mixed woodland to the 'clachan'. Follow the signpost for a good viewpoint to see Schiehallion and Loch Tummel. Return to the track and continue upwards; the way in summer is lined with flowers. Follow the frequent red and yellow waymarks. When the yellow route goes off to the right, continue with the red waymarks up the main track. When the red route leaves the forest road, which turns sharply uphill to the left, stay on the ascending forestry track, leaving the waymarks behind.

3. The track winds first left and then right uphill to a magnificent view across open countryside to Beinn A'Ghlo. Walk on through the acres of conifers and then a newly clear-felled hillside opens up wide, glorious views of the mountains opposite. Bear left at the T-junction and continue until you reach Lochan na Leathain. Pause here and enjoy the reed fringed pool. Beyond the lochan the track comes close to extensive heather moorland. Schiehallion now seems very close.

4. After this pleasing open part of the track you move back into the forest. Go quietly and you might see red deer or a capercaillie. After a gradual descent, a signpost is reached which directs those coming from the opposite direction to their left, and your right, for Loch Bhac. There are two tracks with metal 'public footpath' signs. Take the right-hand one, past a padlocked gate for the short, tree-lined track to the loch. The first view of this lovely sheet of water, with its small boats, makes the long trek through the forest worth while. At the head of the loch lies the magnificent Beinn A'Ghlo. Here the silence is broken only by the sound of an occasional fish jumping for flies. This is the place for your picnic.

*Capercaillie
(displaying)*

5. To return, retrace your steps, enjoying the dramatic views of the Perthshire hills, which appear ahead of you. When you reach the corner with the red waymarks, follow them bearing left into the trees along a grassy track. Very soon the way narrows and the route drops through deciduous woodland and six-foot-high bracken.

6. On reaching a forest track, turn right. As you walk ahead look for the signpost directing you left to a clearing in the forest and the site of a ninth century Pictish ring fort. Return to the track for a short distance and then turn sharp left when you reach a fire hydrant on the left, just before the next red and yellow waymarked post. This is the track taken at the outset and it leads you easily back to the visitor centre.

Practicals

Type of walk: This is a long walk, generally easy underfoot. It takes you through forestry to lovely Loch Bhac, with grand views along the way.

Distance:	10 ½ miles
Time:	5–6 hours
Maps:	OS Landranger 43, Explorer 21

28

Linear walk from Pitlochry to Grandtully, visiting the Dunfallandy Stone and Clachan an Diridh

NB: This is an excellent two-car cross country trek. The best way is to leave one car at the end of the walk and drive with all your party, and their walking gear, to the beginning, then afterwards drive together back to Pitlochry to retrieve the other car. An alternative is to try to time your walk to enable you to catch one of the infrequent buses that run from Grandtully to Pitlochry. It is essential to check bus times at Pitlochry before setting out to do this; the bus runs only on certain days.

Park one car in the car park at the old station yard, behind the Grandtully Hotel, grid ref. 913531 and the other beyond the entrance to the Dunfallandy House Hotel, grid ref. 946567.

Standing stones

Dunfallandy Stone. This Pictish cross slab, probably carved in about the ninth century, records the conversion of the area's inhabitants to Christianity. On the front is a cross divided into panels of interlaced ornament and flanked by angels and beasts. On the back, framed by two serpents, are figures seated on either side of a cross, a horseman, tools and five of the enigmatic Pictish symbols. The monument is cared for by Historic Scotland. It is set behind glass, protected and preserved for all to enjoy.

Clachan an Diridh. In a quiet atmospheric clearing among scots pine, to the right of the route, a narrow path leads to several standing stones.

Walk 28

1. Walk on for 91m/ 100yds to an ancient monument sign on the right. A narrow road leads to a flight of steps that climb to the Dunfallandy Stone. Return to where you have parked and walk on to pass under the A9. Continue ahead along the road and, when reaching the junction, bear left for a further 364m/ 400yds. Look for the

100

footpath sign to Strathtay on the left side of the road, just before the car park for the Pitlochry Festival Theatre. Walk up the narrow lane to a gate to the A9.

2. Cross the main road with care, and press on along the lane, passing farm buildings. Head uphill through pastures. Carry on up the reinforced forestry track. Pass a huge rock to the left of the track. Look for the clearly signposted left turn, a grassy path that leads into the forest.

3. The path climbs steadily through mixed woodland. Away to the left a tiny stream gurgles and chatters merrily. On reaching a forest road look left to see extensive heather-covered moorland. Cross the road and pick up the well signposted grassy

Scotch Argus

path that leads into the forest once more, where you might see dozens of Scotch Argus and fritillary butterflies flitting about the ride. This path soon rejoins the forest road; follow the signpost straight ahead from the junction. Look for a clearing on the right. A narrow path leads to the standing stones, set among pines.

Juniper

4. Continue along the track and walk to a ladder stile, which gives access to open moorland where sheep graze. A narrow path leads diagonally right with white-topped posts to guide you on your way. Ahead are glorious views of the Tay valley, with Aberfeldy to the right and Schiehallion to the far right. Pass through a gate and continue dropping gently downhill, with heather-covered slopes, forested hills and mountains tops stretching ahead of you.

5. Pass through large clumps of juniper to a gate in the deer fence. Turn left as directed to walk beside the fence. From

now on the way drops rapidly, before and after crossing the Tullypowrie Burn. The path keeps to the right bank of the burn for some time, then swings off to the right through the golf course to reach Strathtay.

6. When you reach the road, turn right and then fork left. At the end of this short road, turn left and cross the narrow road bridge over the River Tay. On your right are the rapids which have become famous as a course for white-water canoeists. If you arrive when an event is taking place, the whole area will be crowded with excited competitors and spectators.

7. On the far side of the bridge you are in Grandtully. Turn right and make for the car park, a short distance up on the left, to retrieve your second vehicle.

Small pearl-bordered fritillary

Practicals

Type of walk: This is a very satisfactory hill walk along good paths through farmland, moorland and coniferous woodland. Enjoy the fine views of the Tummel and Tay valleys.

Distance: 6 miles
Time: 2 ½ hours. Add on driving time at each end.
Maps: OS Landranger 52, Explorer 21

Black Spout and Edradour, Pitlochry

Park in the car park, grid ref. 950576, for the start of the walk to Black Spout and Edradour. It is well signposted and lies to the south east of Pitlochry on the north side of the A924.

Black Spout. A web of footpaths leads from Pitlochry to the lovely waterfall on the Edradour Burn. Black Spout, 60m/195ft descends first in white-topped cascades and then plummets in a very long foaming drop into a dark pool. Finally, the surging white water falls for a third time before racing on downhill. The amphitheatre, over which descends spectacular twin falls, is lined with rowan, birch, hazel, oak, elm and ivy. Black Spout is a sight not to be missed.

Edradour, claimed to be the smallest and one of the most picturesque distilleries in Scotland, uses the clear waters of the burn. This originates from deep on Moulin Moor and bubbles through peat and granite before surfacing a few hundred paces away from the distillery. Local barley is malted and dried over peat fires. Edradour was established in 1825.

Black Spout

1. From the car park follow the signpost directions for the woodland walk. Head up the wide reinforced track and where it branches take the right fork through oak woodland. Turn right and follow the signpost for Black Spout, and walk uphill through the oaks to a splendid viewing platform. This was provided by the Rotary Club of Pitlochry and constructed by Aberdeen University Officer Training Corps in July 1989.

2. When you can drag yourself away from the dramatic fall, follow the signpost for Edradour, continuing through oak woodland where wood sage, harebells, devil's bit scabious and golden rod flower in late summer. When the path divides for Moulin and Edradour, fork right following the yellow waymarks and go up to a wall. Here bear left, keeping the wall on your right, with the burn falling noisily, but hidden by lush vegetation. On your left is a fenced field which usually has a crop of barley, and beyond, a fine view of Ben Vrackie. (After visiting the waterfall you may wish to visit the distillery).

3. To continue the walk, leave the path, turn right to carry on for 46m/50yds along the

Goldenrod

narrow road in front of the distillery and turn right again to an access road that leads to Colivoulin farm. Continue past the dwelling and follow the waymark through a gate and along a path. This leads to a kissing gate into Black Spout Wood once again, and on through the trees to a footbridge over the Edradour. Follow the signpost back to the viewing platform for another look at the magnificent falls. Then retrace your outward route to the car park.

Primroses, wood sorrel and golden saxifrage

Practicals

Type of walk: A short walk through mainly oak woodland and pastures to a spectacular waterfall and on to view, or visit, a distillery.

Distance:	2 miles
Time:	1–2 hours
Maps:	OS Landranger 52, Explorer 21

30

The Pass of Killiecrankie and the Linn of Tummel

Park in the Killiecrankie Visitor Centre car park, grid ref. 917627.

Soldier's Leap. From a walled area on the walk you can overlook the Soldier's Leap, where the River Garry races through a deep gorge. In 1689 the Government army, led by General McKay, was ambushed and defeated by the pursuing Highlanders. Here one of the fleeing Redcoat Lowlanders leaped 6m/18 ½ ft over the raging burn and escaped the Jacobites. You also pass the Balfour Stone, reputed to be the grave of Brigadier Barthold Balfour. He was part of the General's army and he died as he tried to escape.

The Falls of Tummel. A visit by Queen Victoria to see these magnificent falls was commemorated by a small monument, which still stands on a rocky promontory. Alas, since the creation of the hydro-electric scheme, completed in 1950, the height and volume of the falls has been reduced. To avoid disappointment

River Garry, Killiecrankie

to visitors the tempestuous stretch of water has been renamed the Linn of Tummel. Look for the old fish pass, which enabled salmon to avoid the falls on their journey upstream. In 1944 the Linn of Tummel, with 50 acres of woodland, was presented to the National Trust by Dr G F Barbour.

1. From the car park, follow the signpost directions for the Soldier's Leap and the Linn of Tummel, using the National Trust for Scotland's footpath. Walk past the Trooper's Den. Here a soldier drew first blood for the Jacobites by shooting a cavalry officer, before the Battle of Killiecrankie. Walk ahead to sit on a seat to enjoy the grand view of the Garry River.

2. Continue on through the birch and oak woodland. Bear right to follow the signpost to the walled area overlooking the Soldier's Leap. Then return to the signpost and continue through the pass, along the densely tree-lined path. Walk below the 155m/510ft long viaduct, which was designed for the Inverness and Perth Junction Railway by Joseph Mitchell and completed in 1863 at a cost of £5,730. The 10 masonry arches were faced with bricks, which saved the cost of dressed stone used for the pillars.

3. Stride on along the path high above the Garry and past the Balfour Stone. Continue through a hazel copse and turn right to follow the Linn of Tummel trail. Walk onto the suspension bridge and look down on the steep gorge below. The water is deep and dark, with lush vegetation lining its banks. Glorious beech trees clothe the slopes above.

Walk 30

107

4. Cross the bridge and turn left to follow the signs for the Linn. Walk downhill under the high road bridge with the river to the left. Beyond, open pastures stretch away to the right. Continue beneath beeches and then climb a flight of steps. At the branching of paths, take the lower one. At the signpost for the Coronation Bridge, turn left and walk down to the monument commemorating Queen Victoria's visit.

5. Return to the path and walk on along a fenced area from where there is a dramatic view of the raging water, imprisoned in its narrow gorge. Then follow a lovely stretch of the plunging river, the path passing beneath Scots pine and heather. Stroll on along the path as it moves away from the river through an open area and then on into mixed woodland. Follow the signpost for the Coronation Bridge, a long metal suspension bridge from where there is a pleasing view of the lively burn. Do not cross.

6. Return to the open area and walk back to the signpost for the bridge. Here follow the waymark pointing uphill to pass through a large planting of Douglas Firs. Walk the airy forest path high above the river, which is well waymarked. Ignore the right branch and continue. Stride on to a waymark pointing acute right. Follow the steps down to a fenced track. Turn right and drop down more steps to cross a narrow stream. Then climb steps and walk along the other side of open pasture, with deciduous woodland to the left. Pass through oaks to join the path taken on your outward journey. Retrace your outward route across the river and back up the track to the Visitor Centre.

Salmon

Practicals

Type of walk: This is lovely walk beside a dramatic river and through magnificent woodland. All is peaceful now, with only a faint lingering atmosphere of the 17th century bloody battle that occurred here.

Distance:	5 miles
Time:	2 ½ hours
Maps:	OS Landrangers 43 and 52, Explorer 21

31

Ben Vrackie

From Pitlochry, take the A924 to Moulin. Turn left along Baledmund Road beyond the Moulin Inn and follow the signposted directions for the walk. The car park is situated among trees, grid ref. 944597.

Ben Vrackie at 841m/2757ft high is not a Munro but it looks like one and feels like one as you ascend its steep slope to the summit. From here you might spot Ben Lawers, Schiehallion, Arthurs Seat in Edinburgh and the Cairngorms.

Ben Vrackie

1. Leave the car park by the signposted path and begin the steady climb through deciduous woodland, keeping close to a small burn. Follow the path as it moves out of the woodland and then back in among the trees. Cross a footbridge and stride on to cross a second into a plantation of larch. Go through the kissing gate beside the deer gate onto open moor.

2. Follow the signpost and walk on, with a dramatic view of Ben Vrackie ahead. Continue over the moor to a seat. Sit here and, in summer, enjoy the colourful variety of wild flowers. Press ahead

Walk 31

to a little burn, which is crossed where the path divides. Ignore the left turn and follow the Ben Vrackie sign ahead. The next fence is negotiated through a kissing gate and the path continues between two small hills, Meall na h-Aodainn Moire and Creag Bhreac. The recommended route now bears left and drops down slightly to the dam at the outlet from Loch a' Choire.

3. Then the steep climb to the summit starts. The clear path, well used and much eroded in recent times is being painstakingly repaired by environmentalists, and climbs to the right of rocky outcrops and scree. Look for both kinds of club moss growing along the path edge. The climb to the ridge is steep. Pause often to enjoy the view of the reed-fringed loch, the village of Killiecrankie and the hills around. At the ridge bear left to attain the summit. Use the indicator panel fixed to a cairn to identify the many mountains you can see. On a good day the view is superb. In summer, the top is a mass of alpine lady's mantle.

4. Most people return by the same route. But if the weather is good and the moorland is an inviting sea of pink heather, you may be tempted to return from the secondary summit. If so, leave Ben Vrackie by a path leading north-east to the lower summit.

5. Then begin to drop downhill over heather,

Bearberry

110

bilberry, crowberry and bearberry, in the direction of an unnamed loch to the left (south-east) of Loch a' Choire. Aim for the long wall that runs above the unnamed loch and to the left (south east) of Creag Bhreac. Keep to the right of the wall downhill. Cross a stream that links both lochs and on to pass below Creag Bhreac. After a short climb upwards, follow the wall as it drops downhill over moorland.

6. Continue ahead until you pass a solitary scots pine. At this point strike diagonally right across the moorland, aiming for the first kissing gate passed through on your outward journey. Then follow the glorious path through the shady trees to the car park.

Alpine lady's mantle

Practicals

Type of walk: This challenging walk crosses open moorland and then on up a steep hill path to the summit of Ben Vrackie, with spectacular views awaiting you. Choose a good day for your walk, wear boots, take waterproofs and a map. Do not attempt in the mist.

Distance: 6 ½ miles
Time: 4–5 hours
Maps: OS Landranger 43 and 52, Explorer 21

32

Loch Errochty

Leave the A9 at Calvine and drive along the B847 through Struan to Trinafour. Cross the bridge over Errochty Water and continue up the slope past Trinafour House, which once was an inn. Beyond, on the right, lies the gate to a plantation of conifers. Park in the wide area by the gate, grid ref. 725644, making sure not to obstruct the way for the farmer or forester.

Trinafour's Wooden Post Office. This stood just beyond the gate. It was dismantled in 1984 and now stands by the museum at Blair Atholl with the following sad note in the window, 'From 12.30pm on the 3rd November, 1984 this post office will be closed'.

Heathers. Cross-leaved heath is widely distributed on high moorlands. It has large, pale-rose coloured, drooping flowers with pale almost to white on their under-sides. The leaves are arranged around the stem in whorls of four. Heather or Ling is found on moorlands all over Britain. The much branched stems are tough and wiry and the flowers pale pink or white. The flowers are persistent preserving much of their original form nine or ten months after they have opened. Purple heath has slender reddish-purple flowers and smooth stems and leaves. The latter are arranged in whorls around the stems in threes. This is the most characteristic plant of the moorland in early autumn, tracts of many acres being continuously covered by it.

1. Pass through the gate and walk up the forest ride, which in summer is bordered with white foxgloves and lined with larch. The way then passes through beech and on through conifers, climbing steadily, its banks lined with great clumps of heather. Be alert for

your first glimpse of the huge dam that holds back Loch Errochty. Away to the left, beyond the tree-line, the heather stretches upwards but not quite to the tops of the outliers of Beinn a' Chuallaich.

2. Once beyond the dam, the loch stretches ahead blue and sparkling. Here you might see black grouse fly up from feeding on the heather; they settle rapidly and are quickly lost to sight. Just before you cross a wooden footbridge look left to see a pretty burn, lined with heather and willow, tumbling in white-topped falls. Climb the tall stile to the right of the deer gate to pass out of the trees and onto open moorland. Stride the track as it keeps well above the loch, then follow it as it drops gently to come beside the silvery water. Look for the roots of great trees exposed along the water's edge as the level of the reservoir has dropped.

3. Follow the track as it passes a derelict cottage and walk on to a wooden footbridge over Allt Ruighe nan Saorach. It was built by

Bridge, Loch Errochty

113

Royal Navy Engineers in 1965, a solid structure but in need of attention. Now you must make a decision. You can turn back and follow the pleasing track just walked. Or, cross the bridge and find your own way around the several inlets at the head of the loch—if there has been heavy rain the feeder burns may require wading or boulder hopping.

4. Aim for a large walled sheep pen on the north-western tip of the loch. From here there is a good path through the heather which passes through a gate in the recently constructed deer fence and an enclave of newly planted conifers. Beyond this it becomes an easy-to-walk vehicle track running the length of the north side of the loch. Look back often for marvellous views of the western mountains with Ben Nevis towering over all.

5. Soon the dam comes into view. Negotiate the platform kissing gate by the bridge over the Allt Con, and head along the track to pass the huge dam. Join the access road and continue onwards, looking right for a good view of Schiehallion. The track drops downwards to a gate. Beyond stride downhill, with Wade Bridge (now unsafe) to your right. Pass Bridge Cottage and continue to the junction.

6. Turn right to walk back to your car.

Black grouse (lekking)

Practicals

Type of walk: This is a grand walk for when the acres of heather are in bloom—but watch out for the bees. To complete the circuit choose a time during a dry spell, wear walking boots and be prepared for rougher and wetter walking around the head of the loch.

Distance: 9 miles
Time: 5 hours
Maps: OS Landranger 42, Pathfinder 293

Falls of Bruar

The walk starts from behind the country shopping development House of Bruar. Approach either from a signposted turn off the main A9, or along the old road (now B8079) from Blair Atholl. Walkers are directed to use the House of Bruar car park, grid ref. 822661. From this you can visit the adjacent Clan Donachaidh Museum, devoted to the history of the Robertsons, a powerful clan in these parts in their day.

Visitors. These lovely falls, considered the greatest in Perthshire, have attracted visitors for over 200 years, including Queen Victoria, William Wordsworth, Robert Burns and J M W Turner. The burn tumbled through bare open hillside until the fourth Duke of Atholl began to plant the banks with trees in response to Burns' poem, 'Humble Petition of the Bruar Water'.

View House. A stone arch is all that remains of the view-house. It was designed to obscure the view of the magnificent middle falls until the last moment, when you emerged from its walls.

Falls of Bruar (upper fall)

1. Leave the car park by an exit behind the restaurant and join a track signposted for the Bruar Falls. Pass through a tunnel beneath the Perth to Inverness railway. Beyond, a notice warns the public to beware of the dangerous cliffs. The path passes through very tall conifers. Notice the rock formations over which the river falls. Continue past a natural rock arch above which drop the lower falls. The lower bridge crosses above.

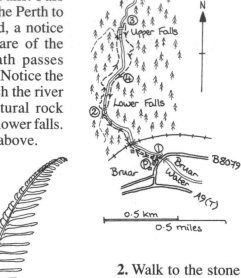

Hard fern

2. Walk to the stone arch to the left of the bridge. Head on uphill, remaining on the western side, passing through dense conifers, festooned with lichens. Large clumps of rhododendron thrive. Beside them grow hard fern with large fertile fronds, standing tall above the infertile ones. Continue on up the wide path until you come to the three arched

116

upper bridge. Cross and press on upstream to the seats by a picnic site, from where there is a good view of the wooded ravine.

3. Return downstream, now on the east bank, and continue to a seat strategically placed for a dramatic view of the upper falls. Four small cascades are followed by a spectacular fall, descending into a deep basin. Just above the pool the raging water creates a flickering rainbow.

4. Pass through the deer gate and follow the notice to another view point and the site of another old view-house. Go on down through the trees to cross the lower bridge and retrace your outward route to regain the car park.

Polypody

Practicals

Type of walk: A short but steepish climb and descent, on good paths, beside a spectacular waterfall—a walk that is a must for all.

Distance: 1 mile
Time: 1 ½ hours
Maps: OS Landranger 43, Explorer 21

34

Glen Tilt

Park in the parking area near the station at Blair Atholl, grid ref. 870654.

Please note: On some weekdays in the spring and summer there is target shooting on the rifle range, during which the public are excluded from part of the route described below. To save a considerable diversion, check with the Atholl Estate Information Centre (01796 481646) before setting out, to make sure the track will be open.

Blair Castle. The castle, for many centuries the chief stronghold of the Earls and Dukes of Atholl, has by its strategic position in the central Highlands, witnessed many stirring events. The oldest part dates back to the time of the Crusader Earl David, who died in 1270. Edward III lodged at the castle in 1336. Mary Queen of Scots

Gows Bridge

was entertained to a 'hunt' in the Atholl Forest in 1564. Between 1652 and 1660 the castle was occupied by a Cromwellian garrison. Prince Charles Stuart stayed at Blair twice and when the castle was occupied by a Hanoverian garrison the Prince's able lieutenant, General Lord George Murray, laid siege to his old home.

Gows Bridge is the furthest point of the Glen Tilt trail. If after crossing the bridge, you continue upstream, climbing well above the river, the view unfolds of the U-shaped, glacially gouged trough of Glen Tilt. This was the old route through to upper Deeside and through the Lairig Ghru to Speyside. The route was used as a drove road by cattle drovers taking black cattle to market. They were driven over the hill to Glen Fernate and so to Kirkmichael, an important gathering point.

Walk 34

1. Walk past the Atholl Arms Hotel and the entrance to the Castle. Continue into the caravan site, which lies on the left. Turn right to take a gate leading to steps to the riverside path. Ahead lies the lovely River Tilt, gracious, wide, surging, brown with peat, and white-topped where it hastens round boulders. This is the start of the Glen Tilt Trail, which is marked with stage posts roughly one mile apart.

2. Head upstream along a good path beneath lofty beech trees. Down to your right look for the York Cascade, where it makes a spectacular leap to join the Tilt. The cascade was named after a member of the Atholl family who was

119

appointed Archbishop of York. Walk ahead for a better view of the waterfall and continue upwards. Carry on across a packhorse bridge to cross over a road and climb into mixed woodland with the Tilt far below to the right.

3. At the reinforced forest track, turn right (Stage one). Follow the arrow pointing right and walk along a narrow path, criss-crossed with tree roots. It passes in a semi-circle through conifers and returns to the forest track. Turn right and walk on, with open pastures to the left and the home farm high above the fields (Stage 2). Leave the cart track by a waymarked arrow to the left and walk through deciduous woodland. This leads to an area of tall larch called Blairuachdar (meaning Upper Blair) wood—Stage 3. Head along the path and turn right on reaching a cart track.

4. Pass through a gate and read the instructions on the board before you progress close to the rifle range. Follow the track as it drops downhill, ignoring various branches going off to the left towards the shooting butts, with the slopes of Meall Dail Min towering to the right. In summer the way is bordered with flowers, including the lovely field felwort. Below, the River Tilt races through a narrows in the gorge.

5. When you reach the river again, cross a bridge over a tributary burn to come to a high ladder-stile, over the deer fence on your left, which you climb—Stage 4. Ascend the recently built forestry road to the top of a rise, where a yellow arrow directs you off right into trees, along a path which passes the ruins of a settlement known as Ach Mhaire Bhig. Soon you emerge from the forest, and the path continues, marked by helpful yellow arrows, across open ground some way above the river, and past more ruined cottages.

6. At Stage 5, walk on to a small bridge over the lovely Allt Mhairc. Perhaps this is the place you will choose for your picnic. Then climb the slope and bear left along a path in the bracken to a waymarked post on the edge of another ruined settlement built round a kiln. The kiln was probably used originally for drying corn and then for producing quick-lime. Go on to cross a small tributary stream and continue to Gows Bridge. The bridge is named after a man who kept a public house when many more people dwelt here.

7. Cross the bridge and turn right to walk past Marble Lodge, Stage 6, which takes its name from an outcrop of green marble found

above the bridge. Continue along the road. Take the waymarked green track, an old right of way that runs above the estate road, soon to return to it. Look for lint pools close to the waymarked post. In these shallow water-filled basins flax, grown in the glen, was soaked to make it easier to work.

8. Leave the estate road on a grassy track indicated by a yellow arrow. Look right to see the truncated spurs of the very steep hills opposite and the extensive conifer planting. Continue along the grassy track, which seems to go, pleasingly, on and on. Walk on past Stage 8. Climb a stile by a metal gate and stroll through the trees of a natural birch wood. After a few minutes, a track forks off to the right. Follow this route and begin the gradual descent through conifers. Take a right fork when the way branches and go on along a grassy path. It runs high above the Tilt gorge.

9. Pass through a gate-way and cross a bridge over a rushing burn, where you might see a stoat dash across in front of you. Follow the track across an open area to a gate to the road, Turn right and walk downhill for 92m/100yds and then, opposite a modern house, turn right into woodland. Walk beneath an avenue of beech, steadily descending to Blair Atholl, keeping beside the lovely Tilt for the last part of the walk.

10. At the main road, turn right and walk through the village to where you have parked your car.

Stoat

Practicals

Type of walk: A pleasing day's walking in a highland glen. Footpaths are followed throughout but the going can be rough and muddy in places.

Distance: 10 ½ miles
Time: 5 hours
Maps: OS Landranger 43, Pathfinders 281 and 294

35

Kirkton of Lude, Glen Fender, and Meall Dail Min

Leave Blair Atholl by the single track road to Glen Fender. This crosses the burn at Fender Bridge and climbs up the valley. Where it levels out a little after a quarter of a mile, a convenient layby, grid ref. 883672, is found on the left hand side, just before the crossroads, where Glen Tilt and Kincraigie Farm are signposted on the left. This is the best place to park, as the return will be by the track from Glen Tilt. There is room for only three cars, so if it is full, drive straight on for another mile to the end of the public road. Just before Tomnaguie farm, grid ref. 896677, there is a large grassy space on the right with much more parking room. A signboard directed at hill walkers explains restrictions on access because of deer management requirements on the estate. Parking here saves a mile of road walking at the outset, but you will have to do it at the end of the circuit to regain your car.

Kirkton of Lude. All that remains is a small, now roofless stone chapel. A curiosity is the modern wrought-iron gate, with the legend A L 1990, which gives access to the ruins. The gate is a valedictory dedication to the Lude family, which long ago lived high up Glen Fender but moved down to Ballentoul around 1650. The gate was consecrated in 1990 and the letters stand for Atholl and Lude.

C.M.Isherwood

Gate, Kirkton of Lude

1. Assuming you have reached grid ref. 896677, either on foot or by car, walk past the farm and on up the reinforced track beyond. Look right to see Loch Moraig. In late summer scabious, harebell and eyebright adorn the track side, and the wetter patches yield grass of parnassus, ragged robin, marsh lousewort and yellow mountain saxifrage.

2. Continue past a conifer plantation on the left. About 275m/330yds beyond look for two iron fence posts set in boulders. Turn right at the second of these down a winding grassy track that makes for a simple restored cottage. The ruins of Kirkton of Lude are a few steps beyond, down on the right.

3. When you have had time to absorb the stillness and the lingering atmosphere of medieval devoutness return to the main track and turn right. As you ascend steadily with the towering massif of

123

Snipe

Beinn A'Ghlo and its satellites ahead, look for a narrow track going up the hill to your left. This starts your ascent of Meall Dail Min. Pause on a grassy knoll, topped by a small cairn and enjoy the widening panorama.

4. There is no clear hill path through the heather. You should make for and cross a fence running beside an old stone wall. Beyond, make for the highest ground ahead, where you might spot mountain hares as you go. The summit plateau is soon reached and from its five cairns there are magnificent views. The summit is the second one reached from the direction climbed. The panorama is extensive. All the high hills surrounding Glen Tilt seem to be close and deceptively accessible. The elusive summit ridge of Beinn A'Ghlo appears between its more forward outriders to the east. Ahead, to the west, the distant summits stretch from Ben Lawers to Ben Alder and, on a clear day, the jagged outline of the Glencoe mountains fills the gap on the horizon opened by the central trough of the Tummel Valley and Rannoch Moor.

5. To descend, go to the last cairn, from which you can make out a largely grassy route down a steady slope southwards, between tracts of heather, with a few rocky outcrops. Make for a fence crossing the hill ahead, which is

Devil's bit scabious and Grass of Parnassus

124

joined by another coming from below you on the right. At the junction there is a sliding wooden gate. Pass through and go carefully down the steep grassy hillside towards Glen Tilt, keeping between the fence dividing off the rest of the hill and a burn which has, through time, eroded quite a deep trough as it tumbles down to the glen.

6. When you reach the Glen Tilt track, turn left, cross the stile and continue straight along the upper track past the end of the woodland. A further stile leads on to the road out of Kincraigie farm on your left. Follow this road to the crossroads. Your car is either in the layby to your right, or a further mile's walk up the road to your left.

Practicals

Type of walk: A satisfying walk deep into a lovely glen, followed by some exciting hill climbing. The return is through Glen Tilt.

Distance: 6 miles
Time: 3 hours
Maps: OS Landranger 43, Pathfinder 294

Kindrogan Hill Trail

The trail starts from Kindrogan Field Centre. To reach the centre leave the A924 at Enochdhu. Follow the well signposted reinforced track to cross the bridge over the River Ardle and on to the car park in the grounds of Kindrogan House, grid ref. 055629.

Pine Marten The pine marten, or marten cat, was formerly a common woodland animal, and in the Middle Ages 'hunting the mart' was almost a national pastime. It was hunted by groups of men on foot with sticks and stones. But the real reduction of its numbers came in the 19th century, when gamekeepers were paid high prices for marten skins. Pine martens, dark-furred and bushy tailed, are occasionally seen racing across the track near the bridge over the River Ardle. Look for a glimpse of one among the trees, or high up in the branches, as you climb.

Bridge at Kindrogan

Kindrogan. The oldest part of the house was built soon after 1700 by William Small. During the 19th century a new frontage and wings were added. Queen Victoria stopped on several occasions at Kindrogan on her extensive travels through the Highlands and after a visit in October 1866, she records in her diary how much she enjoyed a tea-party by the River Ardle. In 1960 the estate was sold to the Forestry Commission. In 1963 Kindrogan was purchased by the Scottish Field Studies Association for use as a residential field centre.

Walk 36

1. Walk back and turn left along the reinforced road taken on your way in. At East Lodge, take the forestry road on the right for 46m/50yds. Look for the narrow footpath on the right (marker post 1). Climb the narrow path uphill between conifers and birch. Head into a dense plantation of larch and fir, past post 2. As the path continues to climb, look for liverworts covering the damper areas.

2. Cross the forest ride. Keep ahead and follow the faint waymark, to pass post 3. Go on to climb the steep way through a tunnel of conifers. Post 4 is found in a compartment of tall larch. Near post 5 boletus fungus grows. Continue past post 6, avoiding huge boulders that lie athwart the path, to a clearing where post 7 is found. Follow the black arrow, which directs you up a very muddy part of the trail. The wet area is soon left behind and the path passes through another dark tunnel created by tall conifers. Continue climbing into a part of the trail where the trees are younger and there is more light. Leave the path and turn right to walk to a raised clearing, where heather covers outcrops of schist. From here there is a grand view of the surrounding heights.

3. Return to the path turn right and walk along the path uphill. Follow the arrow directing you to bear left. Pass the next post and enter another heather-clad clearing where deer tracks mark the path. Then

127

follow the path over a vast area of heather and bilberry to the trig point on Kindrogan Hill (460m/1485ft) and post 9. Enjoy the magnificent view of the Perthshire hills. Look ahead to see Loch Curran with its red-roofed boathouse. To the east looms Mount Blair, to the west lies Ben Vrackie, and Glas Maol stands to the north-east.

4. Stand facing Loch Curran and post 9 and take the path heading right, through the heather to post 10. Follow the track into the trees and begin the gradual drop downhill to pass almost immediately into a clearing. Walk on to the side of a wall, to the right, as you descend. From now on, the way passes regularly from one side of the wall to the other, downhill to where progress is easier. Cross a wet area on rocks and brushwood to pass post 13.

Pine marten

5. At the bottom of the slope, ford a small stream and climb the slope ahead to follow an arrow directing you right. Stride the grassy way, with the stream to your right, to reach a forest road. Turn right at post 14 and right again when you reach the forest road to continue past a reeded pond. Stride on along the track passing through an avenue of beech and lime.

6. Turn left into the main entrance of the field centre.

Practicals

Type of walk. This is a splendid hill trail. Parts of it are fairly steep and parts are muddy. Walking boots required. At the date of publication the descent route has been affected by forestry work. It may for some time be necessary to follow marked diversions to avoid sections blocked by tree-felling.

Distance: 4 miles
Time: 3 hours
Maps: OS Landranger 43, Pathfinder 295

Mount Blair

Park in a layby, grid ref. 155643. To reach this leave the A93 and drive along the B951 past Cray Church. Continue uphill to pass through conifer plantings on either side of the road. The layby lies on the left at the end of the trees.

Mount Blair (744m/2456ft) stands sentinel almost at the start of Glen Shee, separating it from Glenisla. It is an exhilarating, massive easy-to-climb hill, sadly now topped with a large steel tower.

Cowberry and **Bilberry** both belong to the Heath family. Bilberry has delicious black edible fruits. It has several names: Whortleberry in the south, Blaeberry in Scotland, Bilberry in the north of England. It flowers April to May and is found on heaths and moors. Cowberry has evergreen leaves, a creeping habit, whitish flowers. Its edible fruit turn red when ripe.

Cairn on Mount Blair

1. Cross the road, pass through the gate and begin the steady climb. Keep to the left of a small stream, which is hidden from sight in a narrow gutter but noisily makes its way downhill. Head steadily upwards to a metal gate in the fence.

2. Beyond, walk uphill through heather and bilberry. As you climb the heather is less tall, and cowberry grows on bare patches between the plants. When you think you are at the top, you find you have two more large humps of Mount Blair to ascend. Look back often for a magical view up Glen Shee and on into Glen Lochsie. Away to the right the conical shape of Schiehallion stands proud.

3. Continue to the summit cairn and the trig point. Stroll around the flattish top and enjoy the spectacular views of range after range of mountains, stretching away in all directions. The trig point lies in Angus but the cairn in Perthshire and the boundary between the two districts divides these two man-made objects. You have ascended on the Angus side. Since the foregoing was written for the first edition, progress has decreed the installation of a third and much more prominent man-made object at the summit: a large steel tower carrying signals for a mobile telephone company. Whilst the object rather spoils the scale and solitude of the hilltop, by standing with your back to it, you can still enjoy the wonderful views.

130

4. To descend, start from the cairn on the Perthshire side, following a narrow path by the boundary fence down in a northward direction, keeping to the left of it. The fence eventually veers to the right and, soon after, you reach a pair of hurdles at right angles. Cross the hurdle ahead of you, and continue down with the fence on your right until you reach the high clear fence surrounding a plantation. Here cross the fence you have been following and walk round to the right until you reach a hurdle leading to a steeply sloping mossy meadow. Climb this hurdle and go down with the plantation on your left to the gate at the road, opposite your car in the layby.

Cowberry

Practicals

Type of walk: A splendid hill climb—perhaps one from which to see the sun rise.

Distance: 2 ½ miles
Time: 2 hours
Maps: OS Landranger 43, Pathfinder 295

38

Loch Beanie

Leave the A93 at Dalhenzean, 2 miles south of Spittal of Glenshee on a narrow minor road signposted Invereddrie and Compass Christian Centre, Glenshee Lodge. After a quarter of a mile, park on the left verge, grid ref. 133682, just beyond the bridge over Shee Water.

Common Snipe. When disturbed the snipe dashes into the air with a loud, harsh call and begins a zig-zag flight. It spends much of the day in some marshy area or by water where there is thick cover. It feeds on worms, probing the ooze with its long bill which act like flexible forceps. Listen for its strange 'drumming' frequently, but not always, heard during the breeding season. The

Loch Beanie

bird rises with rapid wing beats in towering circles, alternated with sharp descents. As it drops air causes the tail feathers to vibrate.

Walk 38

1. Walk the farm track to Invereddrie. In summer the way is lined with flowers, including the lovely purple and yellow mountain pansy. Pass through a gate and continue beside a stream lined, in summer, with yellow balsam. Here snipe often fly up from the muddy ooze and settle a little further off in another damp area.

2. Where the track swings right to the farm, bear left towards a renovated cottage with a conservatory built on to it. Strike off right just before its gate, and go behind it up to a gate and a wire fence. Beyond this, a little used farm track takes you ahead for some distance and then bends back, climbing towards a metal gate in the next fence. Continue upwards, making for a lone tree to the right of a line of birches, where the fading track goes through a tumbledown wall. It then continues over the boulder-strewn moor, with the Allt Mor below to the right, becoming less distinct but still visible over the sometimes boggy terrain.

3. Follow the path as it drops down the side of a glacial moraine to cross the wooden footbridge just below the confluence of the Allt an Daimh and the Alt Mor. From here stride over the good track to Loch Beanie. Enjoy the oblong-shaped upland loch, with its tiny island and reed-fringed margins, set in the heart of the hills. Grassy slopes covered with rocky outcrops enfold the loch and beyond tower the mountains of Caenlochan Forest.

4. To return, retrace your steps. Cross the bridge and bear right to pick up a good cart track. This leads over the moorland, dropping

133

gently all the way. Just before a deer gate, bear left along a second cart track and through another deer gate. Beyond are grand views to quiet hill farms where sheep graze.

5. The track passes through first a wooden gate and then lower down, a metal gate which leads to the last section. It passes through a stand of scots pine, skirting beside Glenshee Lodge, an outdoor adventure Christian centre, and on round to the layby where you have parked.

Snipe and kingcups

Practicals

Type of walk: An ideal evening walk to a quiet remote loch. After rain it could be muddy and therefore walking boots are advised.

Distance:	4 miles
Time :	2 hours
Maps:	OS Landranger 43, Pathfinder 295

Glenlochsie Lodge from Spittal of Glenshee—linear walk

Leave the A93 by the slip road at the Spittal of Glenshee. Turn into the road signposted Dalmunzie Hotel. Park in the wide grassy area, grid ref. 105701, as directed by a sign addressed to hill walkers.

Railway. The railway was built to take shooting guests from Dalmunzie Hotel up to the Lodge. Look for the buffers, a few sleepers and two small pieces of line. It was scrapped in 1977 and now provides a terrace for pleasing walking along the slopes below Creag a' Chaise and Creag Bhreac.

Mountain Hare. It turns white in winter. It was once believed that the winter whitening of the fur was due to old age but the change of colour is linked with a fall in temperature and provides camouflage on snow-covered ground. It still retains the black tips of its ears. It is smaller than the brown hare but its head is proportionately larger, the ears and tail shorter and the legs longer. It lives mainly above the line of cultivation. It breeds in rock crevices, sheltered from the sight of birds of prey. Two or three litters are produced in a year and there can be up to eight young.

Cheese press

C. M. Isherwood

1. Walk ahead along the road where, to the right, dances Shee Water. Continue to the bridge, beneath which Glen Lochsie Burn and Allt Ghlinn Thaitneich unite to form the Shee. Continue ahead along the road to the Dalmunzie Hotel, a turreted traditional large country house, once the home of Sir Archibald and Lady Birkmyre. Look for the old cheese presses now used as garden ornaments. Head on behind the hotel and walk through a small woodland of scots pine and birch beneath the slopes of Ben Gulabin.

2. Follow the reinforced track deeper into the glen. Look right to see the dramatic Gleann Taitneach, with its tumbling burn, glacial mounds and towering heights. Keep to the track as it swings right to Glenlochsie farm. Turn left by a renovated house through the

136

farmyard, go through a gate and take the estate track which continues up the glen parallel to the burn.

3. After less than half a mile you reach a wire fence with a gate across the track. Continue past the gate for a short distance, then leave the estate track on a narrow path which goes off to the right, indistinctly at first through rather boggy ground. Make for the grassy slope ahead, where a path can be clearly seen climbing between two heather-clad knolls. At the top of the rise, you will see a stony mound, which proves to be the terminal buffers of the dismantled light railway.

4. Join its track, which is your route all the way to Glenlochsie Lodge. From this airy terrace there are spectacular views of Glen Lochsie Burn and lesser streams hurtling down the slopes of Meall a' Choire Bhuidhe to join it. In autumn the slopes down to the river are deep purple with heather. Cross the bridge over a narrow burn and walk further into the mountains. Keep a sharp look out for mountain hares.

5. The railway track ends some way above the remains of the Lodge building, at a short stone platform provided for the alighting passengers. Here drop down a narrow path to an elementary but sound footbridge over the swirling waters of the Allt Clais Mhor. Walk down past the collapsing ruins of the Lodge, cross the estate track and look up the glorious Lochsie Gorge, with its magnificent waterfalls.

6. Return by the same route, savouring to the full the view down Glen Shee.

Practicals

Type of walk: A most pleasing linear walk, taking you deep into the mountains but for once demanding little energy!

Distance: 7 miles
Time: 3 hours
Maps: OS Landranger 43, Pathfinder 282

40

Glas Maol and Creag Leacach

The Cairnwell car park is a vast parking area provided for skiers. It lies near the summit of the A93, just beyond the Devil's Elbow (now-bypassed), the road that connects Glenshee with Braemar. If coming from the latter, park just before the red-painted road barriers, grid ref. 142776.

Munros. Sir Hugh Munro (1856–1919) gave his name to mountains in Scotland which are over 3000ft. In 1889 he became a founder member of the Scottish Mountaineering Club (SMC). He was familiar with the Scottish hills and soon realised that there were more mountains over 3000ft than had been previously recognised. His list of 277 'Munros' appeared in the first volume of the SMC journal in 1891. Once Munro-bagging was a pastime for professional and titled people. Now people of all ages and all occupations enjoy the challenge of completing all the 284 Munros, the latest number of mountains considered to be over 3000ft. In this walk two can be added to your list.

Creag Leacach from Meall Odhar

1. Leave the back of the parking area by a reinforced track that rises steeply, keeping to the left of a mound. The way then dips into a hollow where, in summer, the buildings at the foot of the ski-tows appear very unloved. Continue steadily upwards, keeping to the right of the ski-tow. Notice as you go the Caenlochan Nature Reserve board. The legend reminds you that you are in an area of alpine-arctic vegetation that is extremely fragile and easily damaged. It says the vegetation is very slow growing and takes many years to recover from damage.

2. Walk on upwards and look out for ptarmigan and golden plover as you go. Continue to the top of Meall Odhar (923m/3025ft). It has a grassy summit littered with outcrops of rock and covered with huge patches of alpine lady's mantle. Walk ahead (south-west), dropping down from the summit to cross a wide grassy col between two deep corries. Pass another nature reserve board. Follow the good path that gradually ascends the lower slopes of Glas Maol.

Chickweed wintergreen

3. On reaching the ridge look out for the old fence posts, part of the county boundary between Aberdeenshire, Angus and Perthshire. Then bear south-east to attain the summit (1063m/3503ft). Pause here and enjoy the magnificent view.

4. Leave the summit by heading south-west down an obvious spur, treading the pleasing mountain turf to reach a prominent shelter of rocks, marked as a cairn on the OS map. Look for the delicate chickweed wintergreen growing here in a wet area. Stride on, keeping to the right of a low wall that continues all the way to the summit of Creag Leacach. Look over the wall, as you go, to see far below the stream in Glen Brighty, hurrying downhill.

5. The view from the summit (987m/3238ft) is stupendous—a peak surrounded by other lofty peaks. Continue to the most southerly point of Creag Leacach. Here follow a narrow path that swings right below the cairned top, and descend to the edge of the scree. Then go down to the col before Meall Gorm and on over grass to a stream. Continue on the long descent keeping Meall Gorm to the left.

6. Cross the stream in the valley bottom on convenient boulders and climb up the slope ahead, bearing to the left to pick up a good path. On joining it, climb steadily uphill for a grand airy walk. To the left, far below, lies the Devil's Elbow. To the right, high above, see the route taken earlier. The path eventually becomes a track and in turn joins the track taken at the start of the walk at the mound below the nature reserve board.

7. Turn left and walk down the long track to the car park.

Golden plover

Practicals

Type of walk: This is an exhilarating nine mile walk. The track at the start is rough and contrasts sharply with the springy grassy top of Glas Maol. The way down below Meall Gorm is arduous but it does provide a satisfactory alternative to walking one-and-a-half miles of the A93 to the car park.

Distance:	9 miles
Time:	6–7 hours
Maps:	OS Landranger 43, Pathfinder 282, Harveys Superwalker Lochnagar & Glenshee (1-25,000)

Clan Walks

A series of walks described by Mary Welsh, covering some of the most popular holiday areas in the Scottish Highlands and Islands.

Titles published so far include:

1. 44 WALKS ON THE ISLE OF ARRAN
2. WALKS ON THE ISLE OF SKYE
3. WALKS IN WESTER ROSS
4. WALKS IN PERTHSHIRE
5. WALKS IN THE WESTERN ISLES
6. WALKS IN ORKNEY
7. WALKS ON SHETLAND
8. WALKS ON ISLAY
9. WALKS ON CANNA, RUM, EIGG & MULL
10. WALKS ON TIREE, COLL, COLONSAY AND A TASTE OF MULL
11. WALKS IN DUMFRIES AND GALLOWAY

OTHER TITLES IN PREPARATION

Books in this series can be ordered through booksellers anywhere. In the event of difficulty write to Clan Books, The Cross, DOUNE, FK16 6BE, Scotland.